C0-ALR-847

Raising Ravenous Readers

Activities to Create a
Lifelong Appetite for Reading

Written by Linda Schwartz
Illustrated by Kathy Parks

The Learning Works

Cover Design and Illustration:
  Kathy Parks

Text Design and Editorial Production:
  Clark Editorial & Design

All rights reserved. No form of this work may be reproduced, trans-mitted, or recorded without written permission from the publisher. Inquiries should be addressed to the Permissions Department.

Copyright © 1998
The Learning Works, Inc.
Santa Barbara, California 93160

ISBN: 0-88160-309-0
LW 378

Printed in the United States of America.

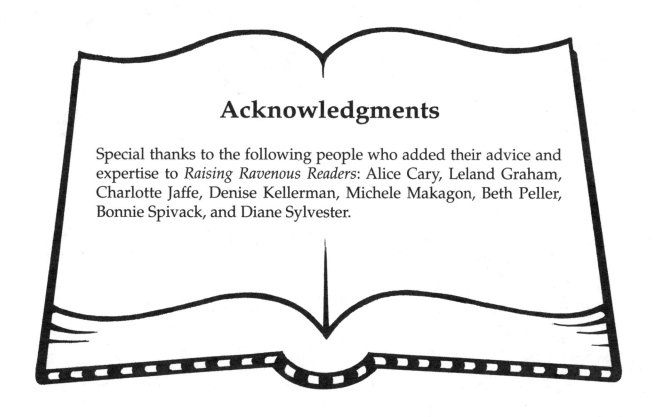

Acknowledgments

Special thanks to the following people who added their advice and expertise to *Raising Ravenous Readers*: Alice Cary, Leland Graham, Charlotte Jaffe, Denise Kellerman, Michele Makagon, Beth Peller, Bonnie Spivack, and Diane Sylvester.

Raising Ravenous Readers
© The Learning Works, Inc.

Contents

Contents

Reading for Information ◆ 69–94

Raising Ravenous Readers
© The Learning Works, Inc.

Contents

A Note to Kids

Dear Friends,

Books and reading have been an important part of my life for as long as I can remember. Even today, one of my favorite things to do is to browse through a bookstore and select new authors and titles to read. I realize that not all of you love reading; in fact, many of you read only under protest. That is why I wrote this book!

The purpose of *Raising Ravenous Readers* is to help you discover the doors books can open for you and the adventures books hold within their pages. *Raising Ravenous Readers* is packed with fun things to search for in books, creative projects you can do when you finish a book, and lists of books to start you off reading about the things that interest you the most. If I can instill the love of reading in just one of you, I will have accomplished my goal.

I'd love to hear from you, so please write and let me know how you enjoyed *Raising Ravenous Readers* and how it changed your feelings about books.

Your friend,

Linda Schwartz
author

A Reading Inventory

On a separate piece of paper, take the following reading survey.

1. How much do you enjoy reading?
   a. a lot
   b. somewhat
   c. not very much
   d. not at all

2. What are the titles of some of the books you own?

3. Where is your favorite place to read?

4. About how many books do you check out from the library each month to read solely for pleasure?

5. What are your favorite types of books to read? (List all that apply.)

- adventure
- autobiographies
- biographies
- fairy tales
- historical fiction
- how-to books
- mysteries
- nature books
- poetry
- romance novels
- science fiction
- westerns

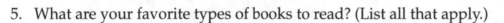

A Reading Inventory
(continued)

6. What section of the newspaper do you enjoy reading the most? (editorials, news section, sports, comics, travel, etc.)

7. What magazines do you or your family subscribe to?

8. How much time do you spend each day reading for pleasure at home? At school?

9. What are two of your favorite books?

10. Who are some of your favorite authors?

Raising Ravenous Readers
© The Learning Works, Inc.

Things You Can Read

Books, newspapers, and magazines aren't the only things you can read. Here is a fun list of other things to read. What other things can you think of to read?

advertisement
agreement
almanac
anthology
application
atlas
billboard
book
brochure
bulletin
bumper sticker
cartoon
catalog
chart
circular
contract
critique
diary
dictionary
digest
directory
e-mail
encyclopedia
essay
flyer
formula

graffiti
greeting card
handbook
instructions
invitation
journal
label
letter
limerick
list
log
magazine
manual
map
marquee
memo
menu
newspaper
note
notebook
obituary
palindrome
pamphlet
paragraph
periodical
placard

play
playbill
poem
postcard
program
questionnaire
receipt
recipe
report
review
riddle
script
sentence
sign
skywriting
speech
story
summary
tabloid
telegram
test
textbook
thesaurus
transcript
verdict
verse

Super Duper Words

Super Duper Words are challenging, fun words to look for as you read. Reproduce the words on pages 12–19 on card stock and cut them apart to make flash cards. Pick a new card at the beginning of each week. If you are not familiar with the word, look up its meaning in a dictionary. Post the word on your refrigerator and ask your family members to join you in looking for this word during the week as you read books, magazines, newspapers, or any printed matter. Decide on a prize or bonus for anyone who finds the Super Duper Word before the week is up. The second week, search for a new Super Duper Word. (As an extra challenge, try looking for the new Super Duper Word as well as the word from the previous week.) Not only will you have fun looking for these Super Duper Words, your vocabulary will grow as well.

adamant	**atrocious**	**banal**
apathy	**balmy**	**brawny**

Super Duper Words
(continued)

brilliant	**concise**	**dubious**
brusque	**dearth**	**extrovert**
candor	**docile**	**emit**

Raising Ravenous Readers
© The Learning Works, Inc.

Super Duper Words
(continued)

ennui	foliage	glamorous
equilibrium	ghastly	havoc
flamboyant	glorious	hindrance

Super Duper Words
(continued)

insipid	instrumental	jovial
instigate	isolate	kin
instill	jaunt	knack

Raising Ravenous Readers
© The Learning Works, Inc.

Super Duper Words
(continued)

lethargic	melancholy	merit
ludicrous	melodious	navigate
magnificent	mentor	negate

Super Duper Words
(continued)

nucleus	pacify	rambunctious
officiate	penchant	reluctant
ominous	plethora	remarkable

Raising Ravenous Readers
© The Learning Works, Inc.

Super Duper Words
(continued)

savvy	tedious	turmoil
sporadic	thwart	ultimatum
taxing	transient	utopia

Super Duper Words
(continued)

veer	wisp	yearn
velocity	wrath	zeal
veracity	x-ray	zigzag

Raising Ravenous Readers
© The Learning Works, Inc.

The Big 100 Homophone Hunt

Homophones are words that sound alike but have different meanings and spellings such as flower/ flour and ate/eight.

As you read, find words that could be homophones. On a separate piece of paper, list the word and then write its homophone. See how many pairs you can find. Record the date you begin and see how long it takes you to find 100 pairs. After you reach your goal, start a new list and try to beat your own record.

Here are some words to look for as you read. Remember, you don't have to find *both* words in the pair—just one—but be sure to list the word that makes the homophone pair.

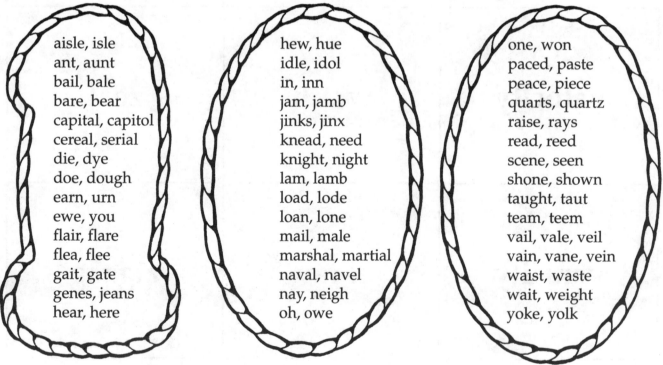

aisle, isle	hew, hue	one, won
ant, aunt	idle, idol	paced, paste
bail, bale	in, inn	peace, piece
bare, bear	jam, jamb	quarts, quartz
capital, capitol	jinks, jinx	raise, rays
cereal, serial	knead, need	read, reed
die, dye	knight, night	scene, seen
doe, dough	lam, lamb	shone, shown
earn, urn	load, lode	taught, taut
ewe, you	loan, lone	team, teem
flair, flare	mail, male	vail, vale, veil
flea, flee	marshal, martial	vain, vane, vein
gait, gate	naval, navel	waist, waste
genes, jeans	nay, neigh	wait, weight
hear, here	oh, owe	yoke, yolk

Adjective Roundup

An *adjective* is a word that describes a noun or a pronoun. An adjective tells which one, what kind, or how many.

As you read books, newspapers, or magazines, go on a roundup for adjectives. Challenge yourself to find two adjectives for each letter of the alphabet. (For more difficult letters, such as "x" and "z," try finding adjectives with those letters inside the word, as in *dazzling*.) Keep your roundup word list on a separate piece of paper.

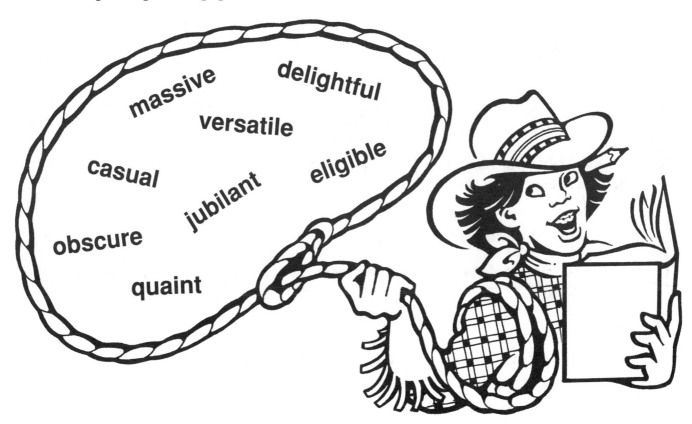

21

Raising Ravenous Readers
© The Learning Works, Inc.

All About Syllables

Here is a list of rules to help you learn how to divide words into syllables.

1. A syllable is a group of letters sounded together.

2. Each syllable must have at least one vowel sound; a word cannot have more syllables than vowel sounds.

3. Words pronounced as one syllable should not be divided.

   dive   helped   through

4. A word containing two consonants between two vowels (vccv) is divided between the two consonants.

   vc cv   vc cv   vc cv
   cor-rect   pret-ty   sis-ter

5. In a two-syllable word containing a single consonant between two vowels (vcv), the consonant usually begins the second syllable.

   v cv   v cv
   po-tion   to-day

6. In a word ending in **-le**, the consonant immediately preceding the **-le** usually begins the last syllable.

   can-<u>d</u>le   mar-<u>b</u>le   gul-li-<u>b</u>le

7. Compound words usually are divided between their word parts.

   down-stairs   rain-bow   sun-shine

All About Syllables
(continued)

Here is a list of rules to help you learn how syllables are accented.

1. In a two-syllable word containing a double consonant, the first syllable is usually accented.

    hap' py   rib' bon

2. In a two-syllable word where the second syllable has two vowels, the second syllable is usually accented.

    con strain'   de fraud'   pre mier'

3. In words ending in **-ion**, **-tion**, **-sion**, **-ial**, and **-ical**, the syllable preceding these endings is usually accented.

    dis cus' sion   re la' tion   of fi' cial

4. In a word containing a prefix, the accent usually falls on or within the root word.

    un kind'   in doors'   re state'

5. In a compound word, the accent usually falls on or within the first word.

    black' board   court' house   farm' hand

Raising Ravenous Readers
© The Learning Works, Inc.

Seven-Syllable Safari

While reading books, magazines, or newspapers, go on a safari to find words that have **exactly** seven syllables such as *differentiability*, *incorrigibility*, *indefensibility*, and *territoriality*. List these seven-syllable words on a separate piece of paper. Happy hunting!

24

Super Sleuth

Be a super sleuth and search for the following information about a book you just finished reading.

title of book

author's name

publisher's name

place of publication

year of publication

number of pages

type of book

summary of the plot

main characters

place and time of story (setting)

25

Hyphenated Word Hunt

A *hyphen* is a punctuation mark that is used to divide words into syllables or to connect them to make *compound words*. As you read, look for the following compound words that use hyphens and give yourself 10 points for each one you find. Challenge yourself to reach 100 points!

all-out	half-mast	push-up
baby-sit	hide-and-seek	quick-tempered
brand-new	jack-in-the-box	quick-witted
brother-in-law	jack-o'-lantern	right-handed
by-product	king-size	run-in
cold-blooded	know-it-all	second-guess
cross-eyed	life-size	self-conscious
custom-built	light-footed	self-made
deep-sea	made-to-order	self-service
double-cross	made-up	small-time
double-decker	middle-aged	thin-skinned
drive-in	old-fashioned	third-rate
dry-clean	one-half	walkie-talkie
father-in-law	one-sided	walk-up
go-between	on-line	well-fixed
go-getter	out-of-date	well-groomed
grown-up	pinch-hit	worn-out
half-baked	ping-pong	would-be

What's Up?

The word **up** can be a noun, a verb, an adjective, an adverb, or a preposition depending on how it is used in a sentence. Here are a few words that begin with **up**:

upbeat	upright
upbringing	uprising
update	uproot
upend	upscale
upgrade	upset
upheaval	upside
uphill	upstage
uphold	upstairs
upholster	upstream
upkeep	upswing
uplift	uptight
upon	uptown
upper	upwind

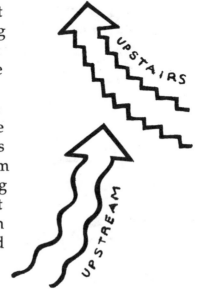

As you read books, magazines, or newspapers, be on the lookout for **up** words. List them on a separate piece of paper and see how long a list you can make.

Just for Fun

Instead of using the word **up**, create a list using any of the following words: **day, ice, down, double,** or **water.**

Raising Ravenous Readers
© The Learning Works, Inc.

Simile Search

A *simile* is a statement in which one thing is said to be like, or the same as, another thing. Here are some examples of similes:

busy as a bee

clean as a whistle

cool as a cucumber

easy as pie

light as a feather

mad as a hornet

neat as a pin

proud as a peacock

quiet as a mouse

stubborn as a mule

Search for similes as you read. Make a list of fun ones you find. Be creative and make up some of your own.

Reading the Newspaper

WHO'S IN THE NEWS?

PLOT THE STOCKS

HELP!

HEADLINE POETRY

CLASSIFIED CUTOUTS

TRIOS

SEQUENCE A COMIC STRIP

BE A SPORT

EDITORIALS

LOCAL ABC'S

Trios

Skim your local newspaper and find three answers for each of the following. (Write your answers on a separate piece of paper.)

Three nouns found in headlines

Three verbs found in headlines

The names of three foreign countries in the news

The names of three world leaders in the news

The names of three bodies of water in the news (lakes, oceans, seas, etc.)

The names of three female athletes in the news

Three movies currently playing

Three companies that are currently hiring

Three animals in the news

Headline Poetry

Find the news section of your local newspaper. Read the headlines for each article. After everyone in your family has finished reading this section of the newspaper, cut out headlines that have interesting, descriptive words. You can cut out single words from the headlines or several words together. Then arrange the words on an unlined sheet of paper and create an original poem using the newspaper headline words you selected. Your poem does not have to rhyme.

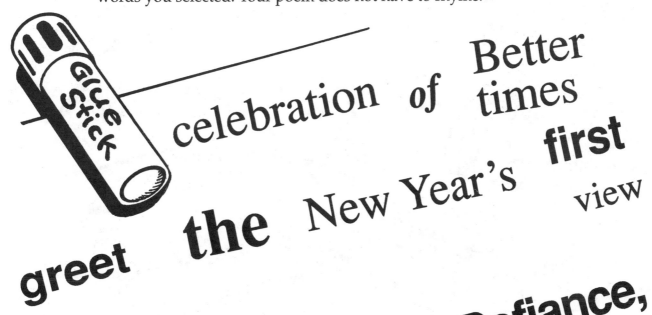

31

Who's In the News?

Skim the newspaper to see how many of the following people you can find. On a separate piece of paper, write the first and last names for each one you find.

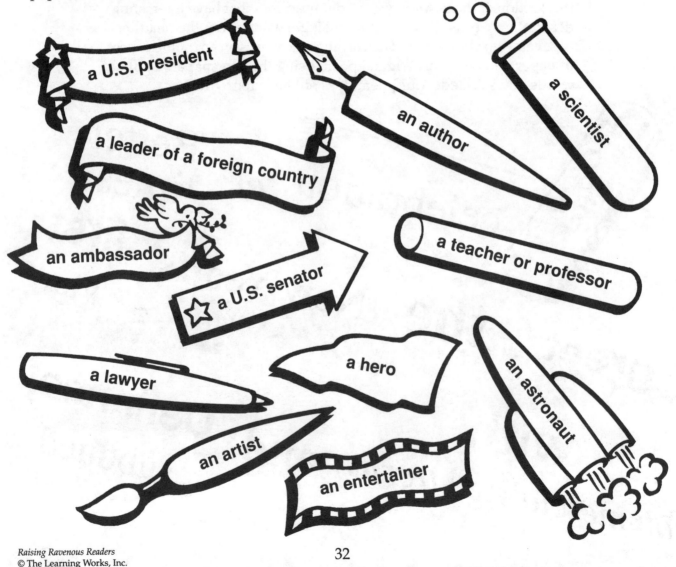

a U.S. president

a leader of a foreign country

an author

a scientist

an ambassador

a teacher or professor

a U.S. senator

a lawyer

a hero

an astronaut

an artist

an entertainer

Local ABC's

The "local" section of your newspaper focuses on people and events making news in your city or town and in neighboring communities.

Find the local section of your newspaper. Have fun skimming this section of the paper to look for the words listed below. (Plurals are accepted.) How many can you find? Try again using tomorrow's newspaper and see if you can beat your own record using these same words.

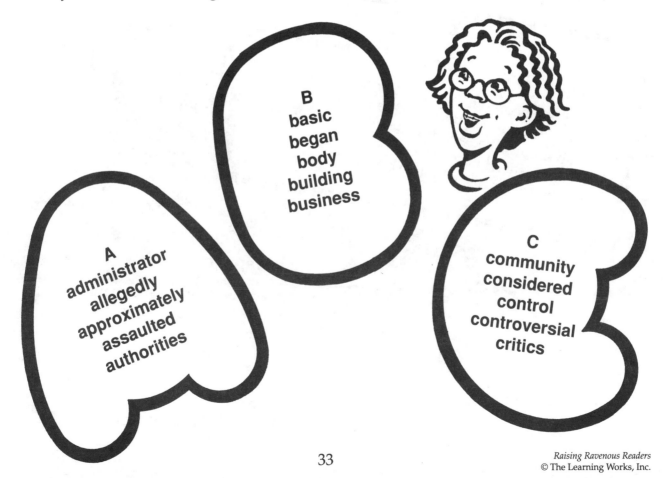

B
basic
began
body
building
business

A
administrator
allegedly
approximately
assaulted
authorities

C
community
considered
control
controversial
critics

Raising Ravenous Readers
© The Learning Works, Inc.

Classified Cutouts

The *classified* section of the newspaper has many functions. One of its major functions is to provide a place where people can advertise or read about job openings and items for sale or rent.

Find the classified section in your local newspaper. Cut out ads that meet the following descriptions and paste them on a separate piece of paper.

For Sale or Rent

- a three-bedroom, two-bath condominium for rent
- an office for rent under $500 a month
- an unfurnished apartment with a pool for rent
- a furnished house for rent
- a house for sale with five bedrooms

Help Wanted

- a live-in caretaker or nanny
- an experienced carpenter
- a teacher
- a machinist
- a cashier

Classified Cutouts
(continued)

Vehicles
Find and cut out ads for:

- a 1968 car
- a convertible
- a motorhome with less than 60,000 miles
- a car selling between $8,000–$9,000
- a truck with over 20,000 miles

Pets
Find and cut out ads for:

- a snake
- a hamster
- a dog
- a kitten
- a bird

Furniture
Find and cut out ads for:

- a couch
- an oak desk
- a glass-top coffee table
- a leather couch or chair
- an entertainment center

Raising Ravenous Readers
© The Learning Works, Inc.

Help!

Look in the classified ads or service directory of your newspaper to find a person you could call if you needed help with the following tasks. Cut out the ads and paste them on a separate piece of paper.

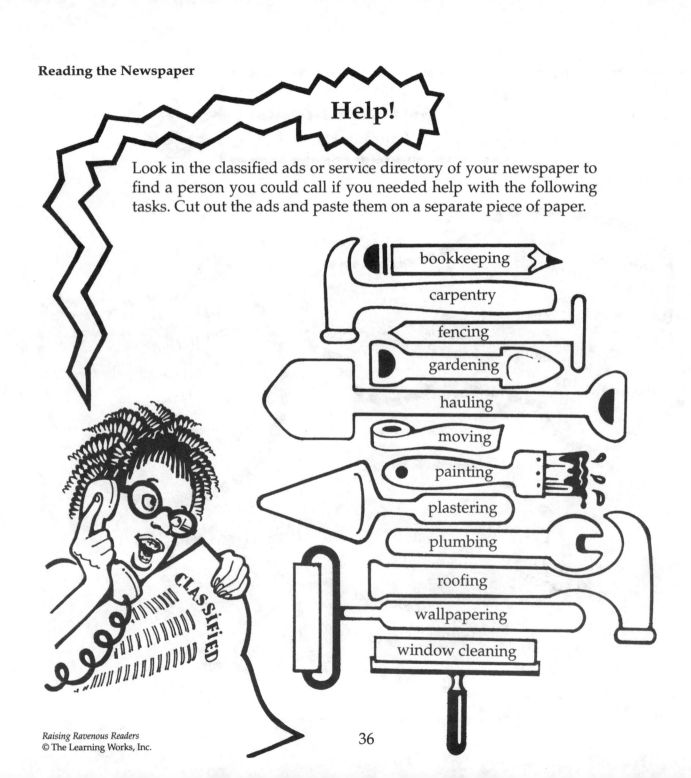

bookkeeping

carpentry

fencing

gardening

hauling

moving

painting

plastering

plumbing

roofing

wallpapering

window cleaning

CLASSIFIED

Sequence a Comic Strip

An important reading skill is learning how to *sequence* or put things in the order in which they happened in a story. Here's a fun activity that provides practice in sequencing.

1. Cut apart your favorite comic strip from the Sunday comics after everyone in your family has finished reading the paper

2. Cut apart the frames and place them in an envelope marked with the name of the comic strip.

3. Repeat step #2 with two other comic strips you enjoy.

4. Open the contents of one envelope and spread the cartoon frames on a table. Read the frames and arrange them in order to tell the story.

5. When you have finished, put the other two comic strips in their proper sequence.

Just for Fun

Create your own cartoon comic strip featuring a super hero or heroine character.

Raising Ravenous Readers
© The Learning Works, Inc.

Plot the Stocks

Here's your chance to learn how to read the stock market section of the newspaper. Start by turning to the newspaper's financial or business section. Find the listing for stocks traded on the New York Stock Exchange (NYSE). This list of stocks is arranged alphabetically by company name. Information is given for each stock, such as the symbol the stock is traded under (its *ticker symbol*), the high and low price for a 52-week period, how many shares of each stock were bought or sold the previous day (the *volume*), and how much one share of that company's stock was worth when the stock market closed the previous day (the *closing price*).

Now try your skill at tracking stock prices. Look up the closing price for each company listed below. To find the closing price, look under the column labeled *last* or *close*. On a separate piece of paper, keep track of these prices for a period of two weeks—Monday through Friday. (Remember: the closing price tells you how much one share of a company's stock was worth when the stock market closed the previous day. Therefore, to find Monday's closing price, you will need to look in Tuesday's newspaper, and so on.)

- Coca Cola (KO)
- Kellogg (K)
- Mattel (MAT)
- Pepsico (PEP)
- Tootsie Roll (TR)
- Toys 'R Us (TOY)

Just for Fun

- Pick four other stocks to follow on your own.
- If you bought 100 shares of each of the six stocks listed above on Monday and sold them two weeks later on Friday, how much money would you have made or lost?

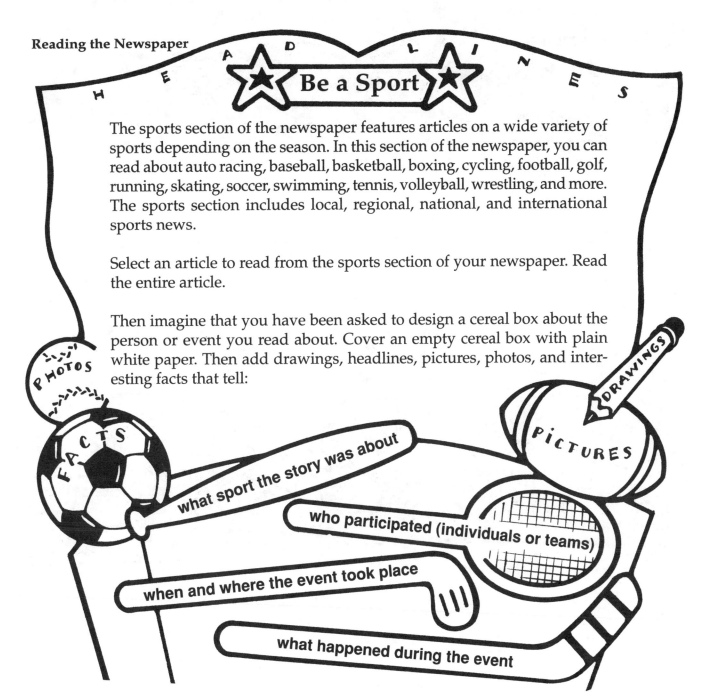

Be a Sport

The sports section of the newspaper features articles on a wide variety of sports depending on the season. In this section of the newspaper, you can read about auto racing, baseball, basketball, boxing, cycling, football, golf, running, skating, soccer, swimming, tennis, volleyball, wrestling, and more. The sports section includes local, regional, national, and international sports news.

Select an article to read from the sports section of your newspaper. Read the entire article.

Then imagine that you have been asked to design a cereal box about the person or event you read about. Cover an empty cereal box with plain white paper. Then add drawings, headlines, pictures, photos, and interesting facts that tell:

- what sport the story was about
- who participated (individuals or teams)
- when and where the event took place
- what happened during the event

39

Editorials

The *editorial* page of a newspaper is a place where people can express their opinions about current events. The purpose of an editorial is to convince the reader to accept an idea, to take a specific action, or to form an opinion. People who write editorials usually attack or defend someone or something currently in the news.

Read an editorial in your local newspaper. In your own words, summarize the writer's opinion in a few sentences. Do you agree or disagree with the writer's viewpoint?

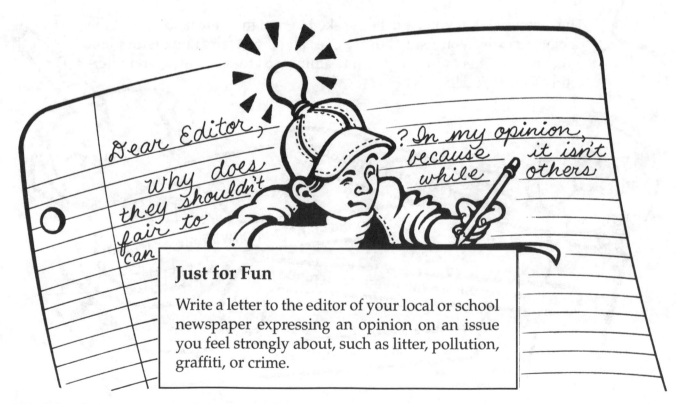

Just for Fun

Write a letter to the editor of your local or school newspaper expressing an opinion on an issue you feel strongly about, such as litter, pollution, graffiti, or crime.

What's Playing at the Movies?

Read the movie section of your newspaper and see if you can find:

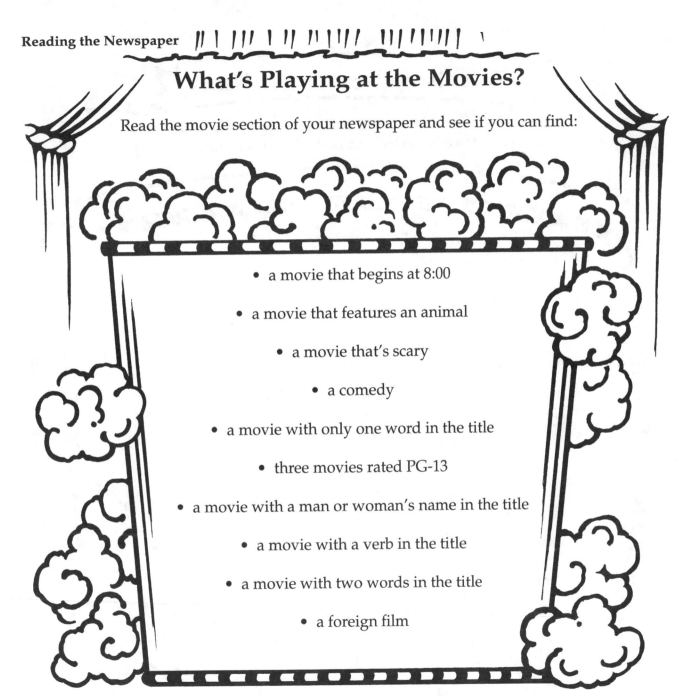

- a movie that begins at 8:00

- a movie that features an animal

- a movie that's scary

- a comedy

- a movie with only one word in the title

- three movies rated PG-13

- a movie with a man or woman's name in the title

- a movie with a verb in the title

- a movie with two words in the title

- a foreign film

Raising Ravenous Readers
© The Learning Works, Inc.

Television Scavenger Hunt

Find the television guide in your local newspaper. Skim through it and play detective to try and find a television show . . .

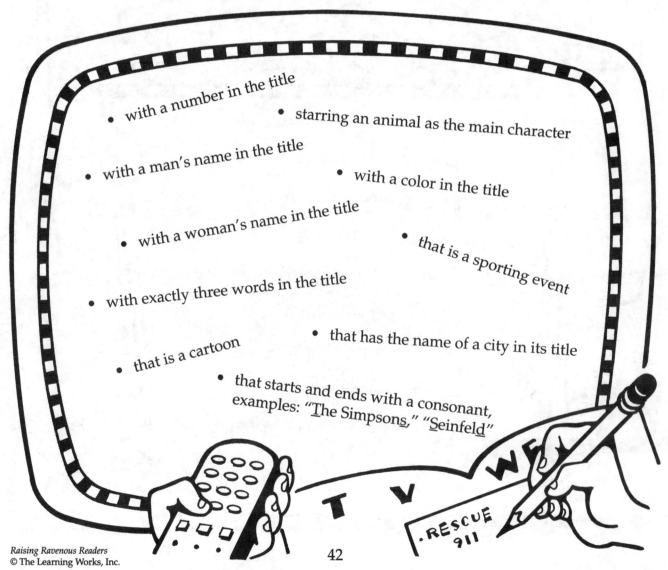

- with a number in the title
- starring an animal as the main character
- with a man's name in the title
- with a color in the title
- with a woman's name in the title
- that is a sporting event
- with exactly three words in the title
- that is a cartoon
- that has the name of a city in its title
- that starts and ends with a consonant, examples: "The Simpson<u>s</u>," "<u>S</u>einfel<u>d</u>"

Adventure Stories

Most adventure stories involve *conflict* or struggle. This conflict can take several forms:

- **person vs. person:** This type of conflict involves a direct struggle between two of the main characters in the story.

- **person vs. nature:** This involves a struggle between one of the characters and an element of nature such as an earthquake, a severe thunderstorm, or a woman or man being stalked by a wild beast.

- **person vs. society:** This is a struggle between a main character and the laws that govern the society in which he or she lives, such as a woman fighting for equal rights.

- **person vs. himself/herself:** This is a struggle between a main character and his or her conscience, such as a teenager who is thinking about lying to his or her parents.

Visit your public or school library and select an adventure book to read. A list of authors who write adventure stories can be found on page 45. Then decide which form of conflict your book used and give specific examples from the book.

Just for Fun

Was the main character of your adventure book a jungle explorer, an archaeologist, a parachutist, a spelunker, or a test pilot? Design a party invitation and plan a party menu based on the theme of the adventure book you read.

Adventure Stories by Author

Avi. Young readers can't go wrong with the likes of *Captain Grey*, about a boy captured by pirates in 1783; *Windcatcher*; or *Man from the Sky*.

Aiken, Joan. This British author is famous for her imagination and daring. Try the series that begins with *The Wolves of Willoughby Chase*.

Lindgren, Astrid. This Swedish author wrote the ebullient "Pippi Longstocking" series about a young heroine who lives without her parents and makes her own rules. Also check out Lindgren's other books, such as *Brothers Lionheart* and *Bill Bergson, Master Detective*.

Morey, Walter. Morey sets his compelling tales in Alaska and the Pacific Northwest. Many of his books feature animals. Try *Gentle Ben* or *Death Walk*, about a boy lost in the Alaskan wilderness.

Paulsen, Gary. Paulsen is a true master of high action and adventure. Try *Hatchet* or *Dogsong*, about a 1,400-mile dog-sled journey.

Need more ideas? Consult R. R. Bowker's *Best Books for Children: Preschool through Grade 6*, by John T. Gillespie and Corinne J. Naden. Libraries are likely to have this invaluable reference that lists books by category and reading level.

Raising Ravenous Readers
© The Learning Works, Inc.

Animal Stories

An *animal story* has an animal as its main character. The animal may act like a human—walking upright, talking, wearing clothes, and displaying emotions such as happiness and sadness. Other animal stories are realistic and true to life. In this type of fiction, the animals behave as animals normally do, such as the dog in the novel *Old Yeller*. There are also animal stories that are based on scientific research. These nonfiction stories recount the actual experiences people have had while working and/or living with animals.

Read one of the books about animals listed on page 47 or select an animal story of your own. Then turn an empty milk carton into the animal character in your book by cutting out pieces of construction paper and gluing them to the milk carton. You can also use buttons, feathers, ribbon, and other odds and ends to decorate your milk carton animal. Be sure to make a sign that tells the title and author of your book.

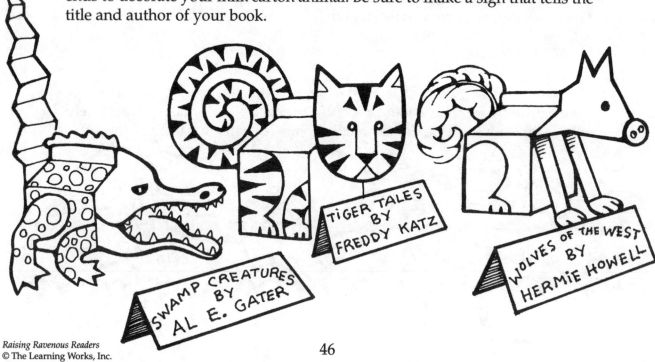

Animal Stories by Author

Arnosky, Jim. Younger children will enjoy the Vermont naturalist's *Crinkleroot* series guide to the outdoors; slightly older readers can learn his *Secrets of a Wildlife Watcher*.

George, Jean Craighead. Craighead is the author of more than 100 books about animals, the outdoors, and adventure, including the classics *My Side of the Mountain* and *Julie of the Wolves*.

King-Smith, Dick. This British farmer is best known for *Babe: The Gallant Pig*, the book that became the hit movie. Try his other numerous animal tales, such as *Pretty Polly* or *The Cuckoo Child*.

Lofting, Hugh. Lofting's *Doctor Dolittle* books feature a long-loved character in children's literature.

Mowat, Farley. Farley is the author of such classics as *Never Cry Wolf*, *Owls in the Family*, and *The Dog Who Wouldn't Be*.

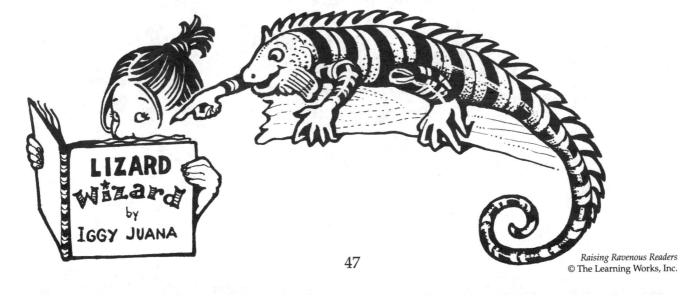

LIZARD Wizard by IGGY JUANA

Raising Ravenous Readers
© The Learning Works, Inc.

Biographies

A *biography* is a written account of a person's life. It is a story written by one person about another person.

Visit your library and select a biography to read. It could be the life story of Elizabeth Blackwell, the first woman doctor in the United States; the life of baseball legend Roberto Clemente; or the story of Dr. Martin Luther King, Jr. You can find biographies of many famous men and women at your library.

When you finish reading the biography, create a diary that might have been written by the person you just read about. Include about 8 to 10 dated entries based on facts you learned about the person you selected. These entries should include important events in his or her life. Have fun decorating the cover of your diary.

Biographies by Author

Freedman, Russell. Freedman is a highly-acclaimed nonfiction writer. Try *Eleanor Roosevelt: A Life of Discovery* and *Lincoln: A Photobiography*.

Fritz, Jean. Fritz's take is always lively, authoritative, and intriguing. Try *What's the Big Idea, Ben Franklin?* or *And Then What Happened, Paul Revere?*

The Learning Works Meet the Author Series. Biographies of beloved children's writers. Titles include *Katherine Paterson* and *Jean Craighead George* (written by Alice Cary), *Lois Lowry* and *Avi* (written by Lois Markham).

McKissack, Patricia and Frederick. This husband and wife team write biographies about African Americans, such as *Sojourner Truth: Ain't I a Woman?*

Stanley, Diane, and Vennema, Peter. This team of authors creates wonderful picture-book biographies, including *Cleopatra* and *Charles Dickens: The Man Who Had Great Expectations*.

Raising Ravenous Readers
© The Learning Works, Inc.

Write a Fantasy Story

Fantasy is a type of fiction that is highly imaginative and often features strange characters placed in unusual settings. Some fantasy stories are set in medieval times and feature knights, dragons, spells, potions, and wizards. Other fantasy stories are set in the future and include cyborgs, laser guns, robots, androids, and automatons. Another type of fantasy story uses animals as the main characters. The animals in a fantasy story have feelings, express emotions, can talk, and even wear clothes!

Visit your public or school library and select a fantasy story to read. A list of authors who write fantasy stories appears on page 51. When you have finished reading, write your own fantasy story. Illustrate your finished story using crayons, felt-tipped markers, or colored pencils. How many words from the Fantasy Word Bank can you incorporate into your fantasy story?

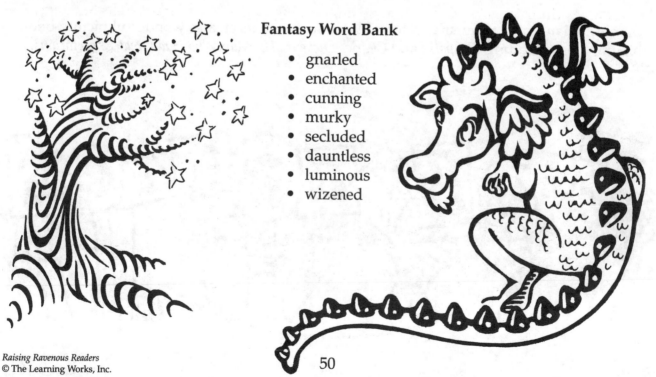

Fantasy Word Bank

- gnarled
- enchanted
- cunning
- murky
- secluded
- dauntless
- luminous
- wizened

Fantasy Stories by Author

Babbitt, Natalie. A great stylist and storyteller, Babbitt's classics include *Tuck Everlasting*, *The Search for Delicious*, and *The Devils' Other Storybook*.

Jacques, Brian. This author's *Redwall* series is a modern classic about the mice and other animals that live around Redwall Abbey.

Lewis, C. S. Children adore the "Chronicles of Narnia" series, beginning with *The Lion, the Witch and the Wardrobe*.

Norton, Mary. This British author is beloved for her "Borrowers" series, about a race of tiny people, and *Bed-Knob and Broomstick*.

Pullman, Philip. *The Golden Compass* is the first of a highly-acclaimed three-volume trilogy.

51

Then and Now

The action in *historical fiction* stories takes place in an earlier period of history rather than in the present. The story might take place during the Middle Ages, during the Revolutionary War, or during the Westward Movement.

As you read a book that is historical fiction, look for examples of how life was different from the present time. For each of the categories listed below, try to find an example in your book of how things were *then* as compared to *now*.

- buildings

- clothing

- communication

- education

- hair styles

- music

- recreation

- technology

- transportation

Historical Clothing

Think about the clothing worn by the main characters in a historical fiction story you've recently read. How was the clothing similar to styles and fashions of today? In what ways was the clothing of that period different?

On a separate piece of paper, draw three main characters from your historical fiction book. Use encyclopedias, the Internet, or other reference sources to give you ideas of the styles and fashions that were popular during the time the story took place.

Then design appropriate costumes of the period for each character. Don't forget to include shoes, hats, and any other accessories that were in style. Color your designs with crayons, colored pencils, or felt-tipped markers.

Raising Ravenous Readers
© The Learning Works, Inc.

Design an Award

The Oscar is given for outstanding achievement in film, the Emmy for the best in television, and the Tony for the best Broadway plays. Now it's your turn to design an award that could be presented to the author of your favorite historical fiction book.

On a separate piece of paper, draw a design for an award for the best book in the category of historical fiction. It could be a trophy, a sculpture, a ribbon, or a medal. If you prefer, you could actually make the award rather than just drawing a picture of it.

Then write a short paragraph describing the book you would select to receive the award and explaining why you selected this particular historical fiction book.

Historical Fiction by Author

Lawson, Robert. His lively must-reads include *Ben and Me* (about Ben Franklin as told by a mouse named Amos) and *Mr. Revere and I.*

Nixon, Joan Lowery. This children's mystery writer is also famed for her "Orphan Train" adventures, beginning with *A Family Apart.*

Paterson, Katherine. Paterson is one of the best authors of children's books writing today. Don't miss *Gip: His Story*, *Lyddie*, or *The Master Puppeteer*, a mystery set in feudal Japan.

Scieszka, Jon. Kids will enjoy the easy-to-read, zany "Time Warp Trio" series, which includes *Your Mother Was a Neanderthal* and *Knights of the Kitchen Table.*

Speare, Elizabeth George. Action, atmosphere, and good writing are combined in classics such as *The Witch of Blackbird Pond*, *The Bronze Bow*, and *The Sign of the Beaver.*

Raising Ravenous Readers
© The Learning Works, Inc.

Create a Joke Book

Unlike a fiction book, which is designed to be read chapter by chapter, joke books can be read in any order. You can start in the middle of the book and then skip around. You can also read for short periods of time and not lose the meaning of what you are reading. This makes joke books ideal to take along to read when you have a few minutes to spare, such as when you are waiting in a doctor's office or waiting for your food in a restaurant. Joke books are great to tuck in your backpack, read aloud, and share with your family when you go on trips.

Visit your school or local library and check out several joke books to read. Create your own book of favorite jokes. Staple about 20 sheets of unlined paper together, and design a cover using colored construction paper. When you find a joke you like, write it in your book and draw an illustration for it. Try to add some original jokes, starting with easier knock-knock jokes. When your book is filled, you just might end up being the life of the party with a joke for every occasion!

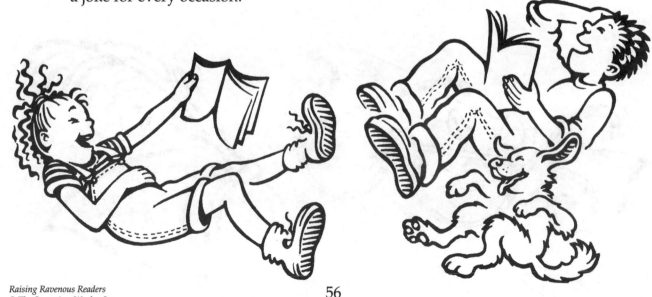

Humor Stories by Author

Cleary, Beverly. Humor and wonderful characters create magic in her many books about such heroes as Henry Huggins, Ramona Quimby, Ribsy the dog, and Ralph S. Mouse.

Dahl, Roald. Once kids are hooked on books such as *Matilda* or *Charlie and the Chocolate Factory*, there's no stopping their devouring of Dahl.

Fleischman, Sid. Tall-tale hilarity is a trademark in such hits as *Humbug Mountain* and *Mr. Mysterious and Company*.

Pinkwater, Daniel. Pinkwater is an offbeat, outlandish writer whose hits include *Fat Men from Space* and *The Hoboken Chicken Emergency*.

Sachar, Louis. Numerous children put Sachar's "Wayside School" series at the top of their lists.

Raising Ravenous Readers
© The Learning Works, Inc.

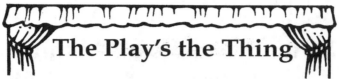

The Play's the Thing

A *mystery* often has a crime (or scary, unexplained events), several clues, and an element of suspense. How the mystery is solved generally is not revealed until the end of the story.

Visit your public or school library and select a mystery to read. A list of authors who write mysteries can be found on page 60. When you finish reading the mystery, get together with several of your classmates or friends and write a skit based on your favorite scene from the book. To make it even more fun, add props, costumes, music, and/or recordings of spooky sounds. Practice your skit and then perform it for your family and friends. Be sure to describe for your audience the events that led up to the scene you are presenting, and explain how the mystery is eventually solved.

Pick a Project

After reading a mystery story, select one of
the following projects as a follow-up activity.

- Pretend that a mystery you have just finished reading has been made into a motion picture. Design a poster for theaters that will entice kids your age to go see the movie.

- Using white art paper, design a book cover for a mystery you have read. You can draw your own illustrations, use magazine pictures, or take photographs for your cover. Use interesting lettering for the title of the book. On the front, inside flap of your book cover, write a brief description of the mystery that will motivate other kids to read the book.

- Write a different ending to a mystery you have read.

Raising Ravenous Readers
© The Learning Works, Inc.

Mystery Stories by Author

Bellairs, John. This American mystery master penned scads of spooky stuff, including *The House with a Clock in Its Walls* and *The Secret of the Underground Room*.

Coville, Bruce. Check out *The Ghost Wore Grey* and *The Ghost in the Third Row*, among others.

Howe, James. Readers will howl with delight and fright at the "Bunnicula" series and *Dew Drop Dead: A Sebastian Barth Mystery*.

Landon, Lucinda. Her "Meg Mackintosh Solve-It-Yourself" mysteries are a great lure to both young intellects and imaginations. Try *Meg Mackintosh and the Mystery at the Medieval Castle*.

Sobol, Donald J. For decades kids have loved to match wits with Encyclopedia Brown, the famous boy detective of the famous series.

Poetry Projects

Take time to enjoy a book of poetry. You'll find poetry dealing with a wide variety of subjects. There are free verse poems, poems that rhyme, couplets, haiku, sonnets, and many other forms of poetry for you to read. Here are some fun projects to do with poems.

Humorous Poems

Read and memorize a poem by Shel Silverstein. Recite the poem for your family or your classmates and listen to them chuckle!

Haiku

At your public or school library, look for books that contain haiku poetry. A haiku is a Japanese poem that does not rhyme. It has three lines: the first line contains five syllables, the second line has seven syllables, and the third line has five. A haiku is usually written about nature and the seasons. It has a light, delicate feeling. Read several haiku poems in the book you selected. On a separate piece of paper, write a haiku on one of the following topics or select a topic of your own: winter, rain, flowers, autumn, rainbows, sunshine, spring, or snow.

Pick a Poet

Learn more about a famous poet. Select one of the following poets, read several of his or her poems, and do research at the library or on the Internet to learn some interesting things about his or her life.

Elizabeth Browning
Robert Burns
Emily Dickinson
Ralph Waldo Emerson
John Keats
Henry Wadsworth Longfellow
Edna St. Vincent Millay

Ogden Nash
Edgar Allan Poe
Carl Sandburg
William Shakespeare
Robert Louis Stevenson
Sara Teasdale
John Greenleaf Whittier

Raising Ravenous Readers
© The Learning Works, Inc.

Poetry Projects
(continued)

Poetry Notebook

Pick a theme that interests you, such as friendship, dogs, horses, nature, or cats. Read three poems on this theme by different poets. Start a poetry notebook and copy the poem you liked the best. Then fill your poetry notebook with favorite poems you read. They can all be on your theme, or, if you prefer, they can be on a variety of different topics.

Match a Poet

Here are the names of six popular childhood poems you have probably heard before. Have fun matching each poem to the poet who wrote it.

Poem	Poet
1. Mary's Lamb (Mary Had a Little Lamb)	A. Eugene Field
2. My Shadow (I Had a Little Shadow)	B. Sara Hale
3. The Owl and the Pussycat	C. Lewis Carroll
4. Casey at the Bat	D. Edward Lear
5. Wynken, Blynken, and Nod	E. Robert Louis Stevenson
6. Jabberwocky	F. Ernest Lawrence Thayer

Poetry by Author

Adoff, Arnold. With collections such as *Eats, Chocolate Dreams*, and *All the Colors of the Race*, Adoff celebrates everything from desserts to racial harmony.

Hopkins, Lee Bennett. This anthologist's collections include *Through Our Eyes: Poems and Pictures about Growing Up* and *Click, Rumble, and Roar: Poems about Machines*.

Prelutsky, Jack. Wit, energy, and imagination make Prelutsky one of children's favorite poets. Check out *The New Kid on the Block* and *Something Big Has Been Here*.

Livingston, Myra Cohn. Livingston is a celebrated children's poet and anthologist who brings poetry to our ears. Her inventive collections include *Space Songs* and *Remembering and Other Poems*.

Silverstein, Shel. Perhaps the dean of children's poets, Silverstein wrote the classics *Where the Sidewalk Ends* and *A Light in the Attic*.

Raising Ravenous Readers
© The Learning Works, Inc.

Science Fiction Fantasy

A *science fiction* story usually takes place in the future. Visit your public or school library and select a science fiction book to read. A list of authors who write science fiction can be found on page 65.

After you read the book, answer the following questions on a separate piece of paper:

- What is the title of the book?

- Who is the author?

- What is the setting (time and place) of the story?

- Who are the main characters? Briefly describe each.

- How is the make-believe or fantasy of the story different from the world you live in?

- If you were writing a science fiction story, describe the setting and characters you would use for your story.

Science Fiction Stories by Author

Christopher, John. His popular "Tripods Trilogy" includes *The White Mountains*, *The City of Gold and Lead*, and *The Pool of Fire*.

L'Engle, Madeleine. No one should miss her "Time Fantasy" series, which begins with *A Wrinkle in Time*.

McCaffrey, Anne. McCaffrey is an Irish writer who sets her novels on planet Pern, colonized by Earthlings. Try *Dragonsong*, *Dragonsinger*, and *Dragondrums*.

Norton, Andre. The author of more than 100 books, Norton tackles racism with *Lavender-Green Magic* and intergalactic travel with *Forerunner Forray*.

Yolen, Jane. This versatile, prolific author wrote a favorite beginning reader series with titles such as *Commander Toad and the Planet of the Grapes* and *Commander Toad in Space*.

65

Sports Fact Cards

What's your favorite sport—baseball, soccer, gymnastics, swimming, basketball? Read a nonfiction book about your favorite sport. You can find a list of authors who write sports stories on page 67. Then, using 3 x 5 index cards, write 12 fascinating facts you learned about the sport after reading the book. Write one fact per card. Draw an illustration on the opposite side. Decorate a box in the theme of your sport. Keep your sports fact cards in the box and share them with your friends.

Sports Stories by Author

Aasang, Nathan. This author has written numerous nonfiction books, including *World-Class Marathoners*, *Winning Women of Tennis*, and *Football's Cunning Coaches*.

Christopher, Matt. This former semiprofessional baseball player has written dozens of sports books, including *The Year Mom Won the Pennant*, *The Hockey Machine*, and *Dirt Bike Racer*.

Knudson, R. R. Knudson brought girls' sports fiction into its own, with novels as well as nonfiction such as *Martina Navratilova: Tennis Power* and *Babe Didrikson: Athlete of the Century*.

Lipsyte, Robert. This sports journalist for the *New York Times* has written nonfiction stories, such as *Free to Be Muhammad Ali* and *Michael Jordan: A Life Above the Rim*, as well as sports novels for slightly older readers.

Tunis, John. This famed author has written numerous sports classics such as *Rookie of the Year*, *Keystone Kids*, and *The Kid from Tomkinsville*.

Raising Ravenous Readers
© The Learning Works, Inc.

Reading Tic-Tac-Toe

Sometimes people pick one type of book and read only that type of book, such as mysteries or biographies. Here's a chance to try some different types of books you might not ordinarily read.

Choose a row below going vertically, horizontally, or diagonally. Read a book in each category for the row you selected. When you finish all three types of books, you have earned a Tic-Tac-Toe. Reward yourself with one of the reading coupons found on pages 138–139. Now select a different row and try reading three other types of books to earn another Tic-Tac-Toe!

SPORTS STORY	HISTORICAL FICTION	TALL TALE
SCIENCE FICTION	ADVENTURE STORY	POETRY
MYSTERY	NONFICTION OR "HOW-TO" BOOK	BIOGRAPHY

Reading for Information

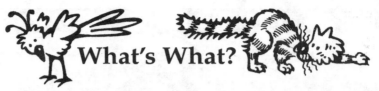

What's What?

Listed below are the names of 24 birds and mammals. On a separate piece of paper, make two columns. Label one *birds* and the other *mammals*. Look up each word in the dictionary and write it under the correct heading.

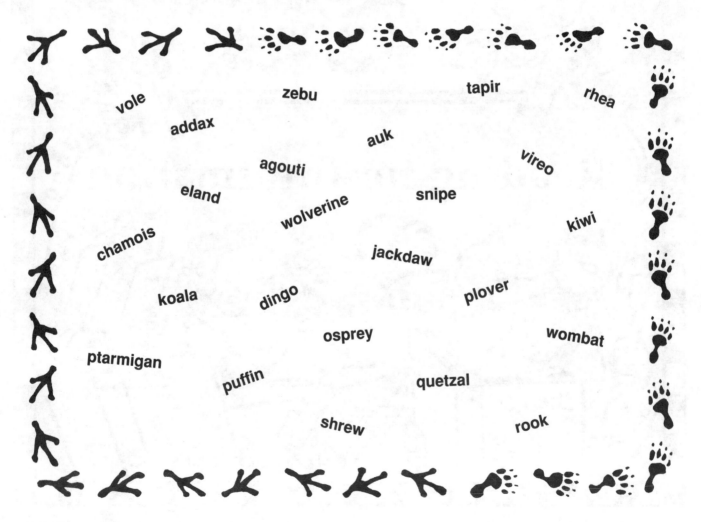

vole

zebu

tapir

rhea

addax

auk

vireo

agouti

eland

snipe

wolverine

kiwi

chamois

jackdaw

koala

dingo

plover

osprey

wombat

ptarmigan

puffin

quetzal

shrew

rook

 # People and Places

Dictionaries contain a wealth of information about people and places. Most dictionaries have entries for historical figures listed in alphabetical order by last name. Using a dictionary, write the answers to the following questions on a separate piece of paper.

People

1. What did Elias Howe invent?
2. In what year was Dwight Eisenhower, the 34th president of the United States, born?
3. What was poet William Bryant's middle name?
4. What important drug did Alexander Fleming discover in 1928?
5. For whom is Chippendale furniture named?

Places

1. Where is Bryce Canyon National Park located?
2. In which ocean would you find the Galapagos Islands?
3. Yokohama is a seaport in which country?
4. Where is the famous volcano Vesuvius located?
5. To what group of islands does Bora Bora belong?

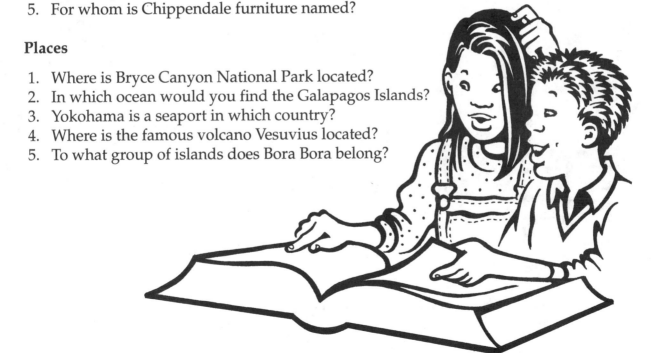

Raising Ravenous Readers
© The Learning Works, Inc.

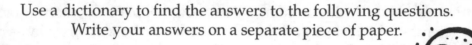

What Would You Do With?

Use a dictionary to find the answers to the following questions.
Write your answers on a separate piece of paper.

1. Would you play, wear, chain, or recite an *epaulet*?

2. Would you row, cook, plant, or ride in a *landau*?

3. Would you fly, swim, ride, or sail in a *howdah*?

4. Would you eat, swing, sew, or plant a *hyacinth*?

5. Would you plant, sing, staple, or eat *zwieback*?

Would you measure, broil, exercise, or wear a *hexagon*?

7. Would you fly, paint, eat, or wear a *snood*?

8. Would you sail, play, cook, or pet a *piccolo*?

Make up your own "What Would You Do With?" dictionary game for members of your family.

◆◆◆◆ Where Would You Find? ◆◆◆◆

Use your dictionary and find the best answer for each question.
Write your answers on a separate piece of paper.

1. Would you find a *bicuspid* in the oven, in a pet shop, or in your mouth?

2. Would you find a *stalagmite* in a cave, on the beach, or in a barber shop?

3. Would you find a *gemsbok* in a bathtub, in the zoo, or in a jewelry store?

4. Would you find a *joist* in your leg, in a tournament, or on the ceiling?

5. Would you find a *clavicle* on a truck, in your body, or in an orchestra?

6. Would you find a *millipede* in the freezer, on the ground, or in a shoe store.

7. Would you find a *chard* in a grocery store, in a zoo, or in the ocean?

8. Would you find a *phlox* on a bagel, in a cage, or in the ground?

Make up five "Where Would You Find?" puzzles for a member of
your family to solve. Have fun browsing through the dictionary.

Raising Ravenous Readers
© The Learning Works, Inc.

All About Encyclopedias

An *encyclopedia* is a set of books, or *volumes*, containing articles, or entries, about many different subjects. In an encyclopedia, these subjects are listed alphabetically. An encyclopedia is a good place to look for information about people, places, events, things, and ideas.

Some Things to Know About Encyclopedias

- When there is a great deal of information about subjects that start with the same letter, publishers often divide the material into two volumes, such as S-Sn and So-Sz.

- When there is not a lot of information about subjects that start with the same letter, entries for two letters may be combined in a single volume, such as J-K, Q-R, and U-V.

- People are listed by their last names rather than by their first names.

- Many encyclopedias have words printed in bold capital letters at the top of each page. These words are called *guide words*. They are arranged in alphabetical order. When you look up a subject in an encyclopedia, these words guide you to the information you need.

  - The guide word on the left-hand page is either the subject of the first entry that appears in the first column of that page or the subject of an entry continued from the page before.

  - The guide word on the right-hand page is the subject of the last entry found on that page.

 **Cross-Reference Review**

Sometimes when using an encyclopedia, you must look under more than one heading to find as much information as possible about a subject. For example, if you wanted to learn about bats, you would look up the subject *bats*. At the end of the bats entry, you might find the words *animal; flying fox; vampire bat*. By looking up each of these related topics, you would find additional information about bats. The words that direct you to look up, or refer to, other related topics or headings are called **cross-references**.

On a separate piece of paper, match the subjects listed below with their cross-references. Write the correct letter in front of each subject to practice your cross-referencing skills as you browse through encyclopedias.

Subjects	Cross-References
1. ultramarine	A. Ukraine
2. feldspar	B. weather (weather balloons)
3. quintillion	C. ragtime
4. asp	D. furniture (the Bauhaus)
5. Kiev	E. lapis lazuli
6. vireo	F. cruiser
7. radiosonde	G. Ararat
8. frigate	H. taro
9. elephant's-ear	I. decimal numeral system (larger numbers)
10. Scott Joplin	J. bird
11. Deluge	K. earth (weathering)
12. Walter Gropius	L. snake

Raising Ravenous Readers
© The Learning Works, Inc.

Key Word Clues

A *key word* is a word that gives you a key, or clue, to the subject of a statement or helps you identify the main idea. Information in encyclopedias is usually organized by key word. For example, if you wanted to learn how to build a piano, you would look up the word *piano* in the encyclopedia, not the word *build*. The key word in this group of words is *piano*.

Where would you look in an encyclopedia to find answers to the following questions? On a separate piece of paper, write the key word or words for each question.

Questions for Research

1. Where was Abraham Lincoln born?

2. On what type of advertising is the most money spent?

3. How long does the average bee live?

4. What is the population of Greece?

5. What are the main holidays celebrated in Israel?

6. What is the only dog that cannot bark?

7. Who are some of Austria's most famous composers?

8. Who built the first heavier-than-air craft able to carry a person and fly successfully?

Encyclopedia Scavenger Hunt

Have each person in your family choose one volume of an encyclopedia. See who can be the first to find each of the people and things listed below. Write your answers on a separate piece of paper.

- a famous woman
- a famous man
- three cities
- three things to eat
- three mammals
- two plants
- two countries
- a famous event
- something made of metal
- an invention
- two insects
- something made of wood
- something that begins and ends with a vowel

Raising Ravenous Readers
© The Learning Works, Inc.

 **Super Trivia Search**

Using the "L" volume of an encyclopedia set, find the answers to these eight questions. Write your responses on a separate piece of paper.

1. In what year were girls first permitted to play on Little League baseball teams?

2. What is Ann Landers' real name?

3. Scholars have counted approximately how many different spoken languages?

4. Laser beams used in industry can produce temperatures of how many degrees Fahrenheit?

5. Abraham Lincoln was assassinated at Ford's Theater while watching a performance of what play?

6. How fast does light travel?

7. What is the state bird of Louisiana?

8. What is Llanfairpwllgwyngyllgogerychwyrndrobwllllantysiliogogogoch?

Just for Fun

- Read about the long word in question 8. Learn where it came from, what it means, and how to pronounce it.

- Pick a different volume of the encyclopedia. Make up several questions about different topics in the volume you selected. Give your questions to family members to answer.

Claim to Fame

Go on a super search in the "W" volume of an encyclopedia to find each name listed below. After you find and read an article about each person, match each person with his or her claim to fame. (Write your answers on a separate piece of paper.)

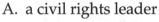

1. Frances Elizabeth Willard
2. Stanford White
3. Jerry West
4. Roy Wilkins
5. William Whipple
6. Jessamyn West

7. Paul Dudley White
8. Marcus Whitman
9. Orson Welles
10. George Westinghouse
11. Ted Williams
12. Noah Webster

A. a civil rights leader
B. an inventor and manufacturer
C. an educator, journalist, and compiler of a dictionary
D. an educator and social reformer
E. a physician and authority on heart disease
F. a baseball player
G. an actor and motion picture director
H. an author
I. an architect
J. a doctor, missionary, and pioneer
K. a basketball player
L. an American Revolutionary leader and signer of the Declaration of Independence

Raising Ravenous Readers
© The Learning Works, Inc.

Magazine Sense

On a separate piece of paper, draw five columns and label the columns with the following headings: **Seeing**, **Smelling**, **Tasting**, **Hearing**, and **Feeling**.

As you read your favorite magazine, find words that are related to each of these five senses. Cut the words out and paste them under the correct headings. Try to find 12 words to paste in each column.

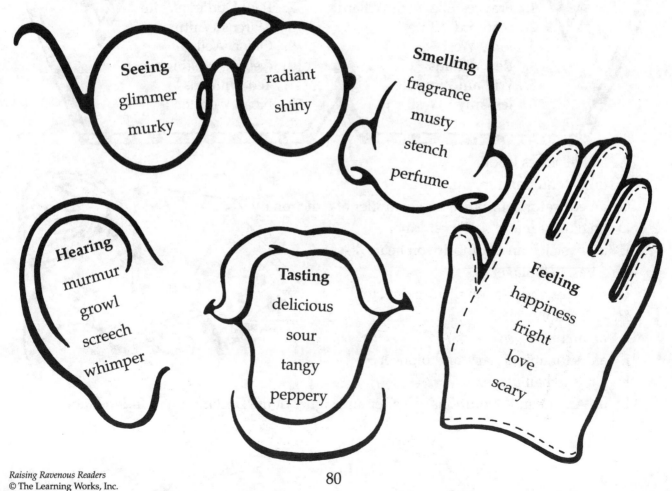

Seeing
glimmer
murky

radiant
shiny

Smelling
fragrance
musty
stench
perfume

Hearing
murmur
growl
screech
whimper

Tasting
delicious
sour
tangy
peppery

Feeling
happiness
fright
love
scary

Fascinating Facts

Today you can find magazines about animals, baseball-card collecting, sports, camping, music, wildlife, cooking, puzzles, biking, rollerblading, and more. So no matter what your hobbies are, you can probably find a magazine that is devoted to your special interests.

Visit your public library and check out a magazine that is written about one of your hobbies or interests. Read the magazine from cover to cover to discover new and fascinating facts about your hobby. Then find a fun way to share what you learned with a friend who also has the same hobby as you. For example, if you collect baseball cards, you might make a chart of the 10 most valuable cards based on what you read in a baseball-card magazine such as *Beckett*. If your hobby is sports, you might make a wire coat-hanger mobile filled with interesting new facts you learned. Write your facts on unlined index cards, one fact per card and attach the cards to the hanger with string. Draw and color pictures for your mobile.

81

Raising Ravenous Readers
© The Learning Works, Inc.

The Power of Persuasion

There are many ways advertisers try to get you to buy their products. Some use well-known celebrities or athletes to endorse their products. The testimonial of a famous person is supposed to persuade you to buy the product. Other advertisers use the bandwagon technique, which conveys the message that everyone else is using a particular product so you should, too.

Select a magazine that has a lot of advertisements. Read them carefully and see if you can find an ad that uses both the testimonial and bandwagon methods of advertising.

Magazine Art Fun

Find a picture you like in a magazine. Look for a fairly simple picture at least four inches tall or wide. Cut it out and fold it in half vertically or horizontally. Cut along the folded line, and paste half of the picture on a plain sheet of white paper. Use a pencil to draw the missing half of the picture. Color your drawing to match the original half.

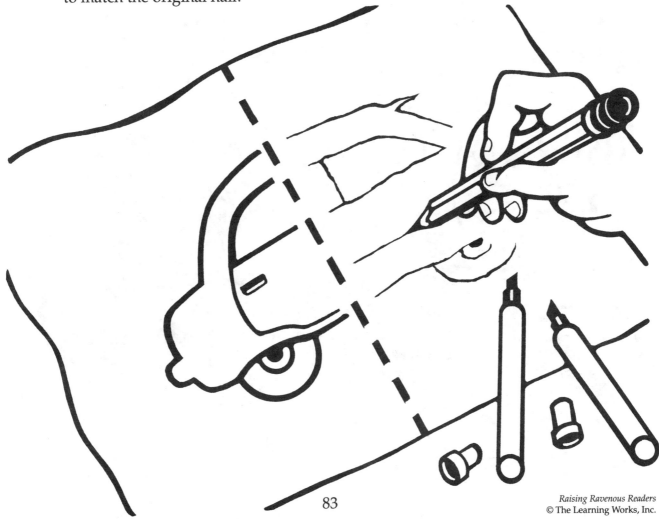

Raising Ravenous Readers
© The Learning Works, Inc.

Around the World

Many of the things your family buys and uses are made in other countries.
Can you find an item in your house from each of the following places?

China

Mexico

Japan

England

Switzerland

Indonesia

Australia

Germany

Compare Nutrition Facts

Pick a type of food that comes in a can or box such as cereals, soups, fruits, or vegetables. Then read the labels on three different types of food you selected.

On a separate piece of paper, copy the following list and make a chart with three columns for the three foods you are comparing. Read the labels on all three items and complete the chart. Which of the three foods is the healthiest?

Per Serving

Calories

Total Fat

Saturated Fat

Cholesterol

Sodium

Total Carbohydrate

Dietary Fiber

Sugars

Protein

Vitamin A

Vitamin C

Calcium

Iron

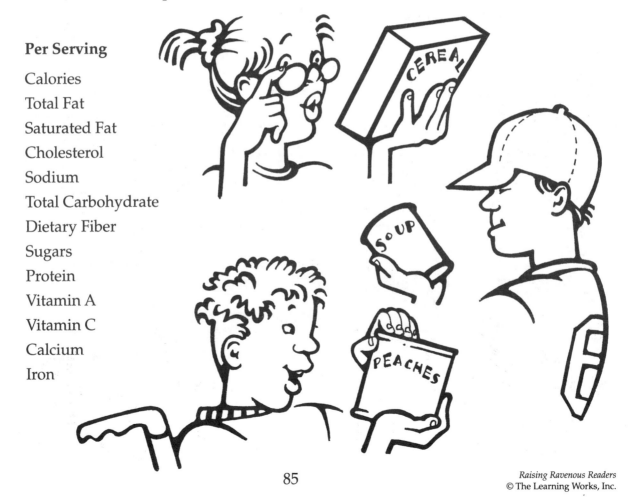

Raising Ravenous Readers
© The Learning Works, Inc.

Reading Maps

A *map* is a representation on a flat surface of all or part of an area.
There are many different kinds of maps.

A *political map* shows state boundaries, state capitals, important cities, and main rivers.

A *product map* shows the main crops, minerals, and manufactured goods produced by a state.

A *population map* shows where most of the people live in a given area, often by means of dots.

A *road map* shows main highways, state boundaries, state capitals, and directions. It helps you get from one place to another.

Other Map Words to Know

- A *map legend* is a list of the symbols that have been used on the map with a brief explanation of the meaning of each one.

- A *map scale* helps you estimate the distances between two points.

- A *compass rose* shows directions on a map. North is usually up, West is to the left, East is to the right, and South is down.

- *Map symbols* are pictures used to represent an item found on a map. For example ✈ = airport, ⌐ = school, and +++++ = railroad

In-Betweeners

Have fun learning to read a map of the United States. Find the state that is located between each pair of states listed below. Write your answers on a separate piece of paper.

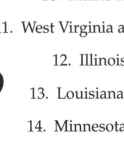

1. Kentucky and Virginia

2. California and Utah

3. Texas and Arizona

4. North Dakota and Nebraska

5. Iowa and Arkansas

6. North Carolina and Georgia

7. South Dakota and Kansas

8. Colorado and Nevada

9. South Carolina and Florida

10. Maine and Vermont

11. West Virginia and North Carolina

12. Illinois and Ohio

13. Louisiana and Missouri

14. Minnesota and Missouri

15. Virginia and South Carolina

Raising Ravenous Readers
© The Learning Works, Inc.

How Many?

Use a map of the United States to answer the following questions. When you are thinking about states, don't forget Hawaii and Alaska. Write your answers on a separate piece of paper.

1. How many states have the word "North" in their names?

2. How many states have only four letters in their names?

3. How many states have names that begin and end with the same letter?

4. How many states border the Atlantic Ocean?

5. How many states border the Gulf of Mexico?

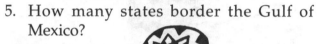

6. How many states have names that begin with a vowel?

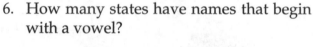

7. How many states have the word "South" in their names?

8. How many states border the Pacific Ocean?

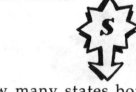

Which Sea?

Use a map or globe to find each pair of countries listed below. On a separate piece of paper, write the name of the sea that lies between the two countries.

1. Japan and North Korea

2. Turkey and Greece

3. Costa Rica and Cuba

4. Israel and Jordan

5. Greenland and Canada

6. Egypt and Saudi Arabia

7. Poland and Sweden

8. Norway and England

9. South Korea and China

10. Oman and India

Raising Ravenous Readers
© The Learning Works, Inc.

 # Read and Eat

When you read and use a recipe to make a special dish, you not only end up with something yummy to eat, but you also learn how to follow written directions. This is an important skill to learn, because no matter what job you have when you are older, you will be expected to follow written directions. How well do you follow directions?

Help prepare dinner for your family one night this week. You'll need mom or dad's help to shop for the ingredients and to assist you as you read and follow the directions given in the recipe. If you don't have any cookbooks at home, you can check out some from your local library. Many magazines also contain recipes. Select a recipe for a main dish, a vegetable, or a dessert. If you're really ambitious, you can cook all three. Gather all the measuring cups, measuring spoons, bowls, pans, and other utensils you'll need before you begin. Read and follow the directions for each recipe carefully. When you are finished, you will be able to taste the results of your success.

 # Recipe Race

Race against time as you search through cookbook recipes to find the 10 ingredients listed below. Copy the list onto a separate piece of paper. Then set a kitchen timer for 10 minutes. As you find each ingredient, cross it off your list. See if you can find all 10 in 10 minutes.

- molasses
- mustard
- onion
- celery
- raisins
- jelly
- oranges
- mint
- brown sugar
- marshmallows

Just for Fun

Make up a new list of ingredients, and race a friend or family member to see who can find all 10 ingredients first.

Look through a cookbook and find a recipe that appeals to you. If your mom or dad gives you permission, follow the directions in the recipe and make it for your family.

Raising Ravenous Readers
© The Learning Works, Inc.

Number, Please!

What telephone number would you call for each of the following situations? Use the white pages and/or yellow pages of your local telephone book to find the appropriate phone number to call.

You want to find out when your local library is open.

You want to reserve space at a local park for a surprise party for your dad.

You want to find out about adopting a dog from the humane society.

You are opening a lemonade stand and want to obtain a business license.

Phone Book Bonanza (White Pages)

Using the white pages of your telephone book, find each of the following:
(For each answer, write the page number on which it was found.)

- the number of people who have the same last name as you

  - a last name that begins with the letter Z

    - a last name that ends with two T's

  - a last name that begins with the letter Q

- a person whose first and last names begin with the same letter

  - someone whose phone number ends with 444

  - someone who has the same first name as you

    - a last name that ends with the letter X

- a person whose last name is the same as a U.S. president

    - a last name with only three letters

  - a last name with twelve or more letters

Raising Ravenous Readers
© The Learning Works, Inc.

Phone Book Bonanza (Yellow Pages)

Use the yellow pages of your telephone book to find each of the following:
(For each answer, write the page number on which it was found.)

- three places to buy pizza

- the name of a toy store

- a business that begins with the letter X

- a business or company that has the name of a bird

- a business or company that has the name of a color

- a business that has a person's name in the title

- a company that delivers balloons

- a company that would sell you a trophy for your coach

- a place where you could rent crutches until your broken leg has healed

- the name of a video store

- a place to buy pet supplies

- a place to repair your bicycle

Parents' Section

Focus on Your Child's Interests

By Bonnie Spivack, Reading Specialist
Arlington Public Schools
Arlington, Virginia

When I was a graduate student in a reading program at Hood College in Frederick, Maryland, I came across a statistic that had a profound effect on my viewpoint on how to best teach reading, especially to students who were "reluctant readers." That statistic stated that interest is 30 times more important than reading ability in determining whether a reader will be able to comprehend a reading selection. With this information in mind, I have tried to discover an area of interest in the students with whom I work.

My quest for focusing on interest came into play as I taught a group of third grade boys who were not only experiencing reading difficulty, but were also displaying a bad attitude toward school in general. They were disruptive and often failed to complete their assignments. I decided to find something that would entice them to complete their work and also be cooperative. I brought in a book which had various patterns of paper airplanes and instructions for making them. I told the students that they could earn a paper airplane if they accumulated six stickers for six days of good behavior and attentive classwork. Suddenly, there was a miraculous change in their behavior.

Not only did they do their classwork but they also began asking if they could look through the book to discover information about the authors of the book and how the different types of airplanes would fly. They wanted to learn about aerodynamics. I went to the library and found books for them about the topic. They took them home and came back and taught *me* about the science of aerodynamics. I would not be surprised to learn if they became future aerospace engineers!

Once we find an area of interest, the possibilities are endless for opening up new discoveries and bringing the excitement of learning to students. As parents and teachers, this is a challenge with unlimited rewards for both the learner and the teacher.

Using Imagination When Reading

By Denise Kellerman
Storyteller
Chicago, Illinois

I am a professional storyteller and have read stories to children in more than 900 elementary schools over the past six years. My advice to parents is to encourage their children to use their imagination as they read. Children today are often glued to the television set or computer monitor for hours on end. They are accustomed to visual stimulation. They often don't take the time to use their imaginations and picture things in their own minds. As a storyteller, one of the most difficult jobs I have is to make children come along with me in their minds as I read. When I ask them if they can see pictures of things I am reading about, the answer, frequently, is "No."

One day I was at a school that had a terrible odor. All of the kids were talking about the awful smell that surrounded the school from something outside. I was having a hard time getting their attention. Out of necessity I began, "Close your eyes and imagine the aroma of brownies baking in the oven." I watched as the expressions on their faces turned to smiles. I took my imagination exercise a step further: "Now, not only smell the brownies, but imagine what they taste like melting in your mouth." My imagination game worked! With their eyes closed and their imaginations at work, the kids were able to actually picture the brownies and imagine their aroma and taste. Years later, kids still remember my imagination game and ask to play it again.

Now I begin each storytelling session by having the kids close their eyes and use their imaginations to draw upon their sense of taste, smell, feel, sound, and sight. Try this technique as you read aloud to your children. Ask them to close their eyes and describe the pictures they see in their minds. Have them try this at the end of each chapter they read on their own in their favorite books. Your child's imagination is a powerful asset that will help him or her get a lot more out of the books he or she reads!

Raising Ravenous Readers
© The Learning Works, Inc.

Discover the WAT of Reading

By Leland Graham

My professional background includes having taught middle school, high school, and college as well as having been a principal. In addition, I have coauthored numerous supplementary teaching books and have worked in the educational school supply business. Through my relationships with professionals in the education field as well as dealing with parents one-on-one, I have developed a clear understanding of some of the successes and pitfalls of the parent as the primary teacher of reading. Among my observations, I have discovered that parents who seem to be the most successful in motivating their children to read are those who make sure their child has the appropriate materials, have realistic expectations, and use positive incentives to encourage achievement.

When motivating your child to read, **WAT** is the answer. **WAT** is an acronym that means reading **W**ith, reading **A**lone, and reading **T**o. Experts agree that children who are engaged in **WAT** on a regular basis are motivated to read, and they increase their reading performance. With **WAT** your child can participate in shared reading activities as they read *with* others or *with* adult partners. As well, children who read *alone* for recreation on a regular basis become better readers. They extend their reading experiences while they read *to* others or are read *to*.

Here are some activities that will help you engage your child in **WAT** and thus motivate your child to read. To promote reading *with* your child you can:

- Let your child select a book from the library that you can read together.
- Form a "Book Folk" group with your child and his or her friends. Encourage the children to select passages from a story or poem to read together.
- Let your child pick a favorite story or poem that repeats phrases. Have your child repeat a particular phrase each time *you* read a new part of the story. In books that don't repeat phrases, read aloud a short portion of a story or poem, then let your child repeat the phrase or sentence.
- Encourage your child to act out the story.

Discover the WAT of Reading
(continued)

To encourage your child to read *alone* for pleasure, you should:

- Provide a variety of reading materials geared to your child's recreational reading level— the level on which your child reads with little or no difficulty. Schedule weekly visits to the library.
- Arrange a time for your child to read, for example, at bedtime. If you are saying time is a problem, keep this in mind: A child who reads *15 minutes per day* will read one-half book per week, 2 books per month, 24 books per year, and 1,000 books in a lifetime.
- Set *goals*. Help your child determine the number of books he or she will read each week; but be realistic. One or two books may be reasonable, depending on the child's age and ability level. For some children, several chapters a week may be more appropriate.
- Provide *incentives* for your child when he or she reads on a regular basis or reaches a certain goal. For example, you could reward your child for reading 15 minutes daily.

Every time you read *to* your child you are building an appreciation for reading. Children may learn the mechanics of reading by having the story read to them. They hear correct phrasing, punctuation, and voice pitch from the person reading. Most importantly, children see you modeling the activity of reading. Try these ideas to motivate your child to read *to* you or listen *to* you read:

- Ask your child to read to you. Set a time aside for you to share books together.
- Choose books that appeal to your child's interests. If a book is above his or her recreational reading level, you can read the book to your child.
- Take turns reading aloud with your child. Be mindful that your child may be concentrating on how to read, and reading aloud helps to keep the story alive.

You can foster an appreciation for literature and create a lifelong love of reading when you help your child discover the **WAT** of reading.

The author wishes to thank Valerie Harrison, reading consultant, DeKalb County
Schools, Decatur, Georgia, for contributing to the ideas presented in this article.

Solving Problems Through Reading

by Charlotte Jaffe
Coordinator of Gifted Education in the Clementon, New Jersey, School District
and author of more than 50 educational books and games for children

Reading can be an effective tool for helping children solve their problems. In classrooms today, teachers often find themselves involved in helping children respond to a variety of difficult family situations, as well as the usual playground skirmishes. Sometimes teachers are the only ones their troubled students can turn to for advice. However, there is another source of classroom counseling available, and it can be found in the Reading Corner.

Dealing with the ripple effect of death, disability, discrimination, or divorce, many authors of books for children present realistic views of the difficulties that children must face in their daily lives. Through these well-drawn story characters, young readers can gain insight into their own troubling situations and hopefully find answers that they can apply.

I always encourage my students to seek solutions through literature. In one instance, a primary student, troubled by the loss of a family member, came to me for solace. I referred her to *Annie and the Old One*, a story in which a child is helped to cope with the death of a beloved grandparent. The loss of a family pet can also be devastating to a child. *Where the Red Fern Grows* is one of many excellent books that deal with this topic. Relationships, growing up, and self-esteem are subjects that often distress children. *Dear Mr. Henshaw* is an award-winning novel that I often suggest to students who are having difficulty accepting divorce or separation from a parent.

Solving Problems Through Reading
(continued)

After my students have read the books, we usually have a discussion about the theme and characters. Many times I include the question, "What will happen next?" I am always impressed by the extent of their comprehension. This level of comprehension has occurred because the students have become so involved in the story. Reading novels to solve problems is a strategy that works in my classroom. It also serves to arouse interest in reading and improve reading comprehension.

For an excellent list of issue-related books, see pages 133–136. This list provides suggestions for books dealing with the following topics: alcohol, death, divorce, domestic violence, drugs, illness, moving, school stories, sexual abuse, and tolerance.

101

Windows of Opportunity

By Michele Makagon
Principal of Escalana Elementary School
La Mirada, California

Parents want their children to read. They know that good readers are more successful in life. I have been a principal for nine years and a teacher and reading specialist for 20 years. The question most often asked by concerned parents is "How can I be sure my child will become a good reader?"

The good news is that all children can learn to read. In grades 3–6, they move from "learning to read" to "reading to learn." As parents, you are important in their continuing development and interest in reading. Some children naturally enjoy reading—the kind who read under the covers at night with a flashlight. Others can read, but show only minimal interest and read slowly, with little enthusiasm. All children need guidance and motivation because what they read and how much they read needs to be monitored by you.

Begin by selecting a school that values literacy. Visit during the reading/language arts program. Observe as much as possible; talk to the teachers and the principal. It is essential that all language arts programs have the following components: a strong literature program, balancing oral and written language; organized skills; regular assessment; and intervention if there is a diagnosis showing a child is at risk of reading difficulties. Confer with the teacher regularly, asking specifically about the reading level of your child. Most importantly, ask how well your child understands what is read and if he or she can apply that knowledge to other subjects, such as science and history. Look for a class library with a variety of books on many topics. Student work in language arts should be on display. Check your child's homework to be sure reading is included on a daily basis. Visit the school library to see if the media, books, and technology are up to date and meet the needs of the children for individual or class projects. If you find a problem in any of these areas, talk to the teacher and/or principal. Express your concerns. Become involved in the parent organizations, such as the PTA, and work toward a positive change where needed.

Windows of Opportunity
(continued)

I tell parents that good reading involves fluency. It's like taking piano lessons. The instructor can teach all the notes and keys, but unless the student practices regularly, the music will not flow in an easy, fluent way, and soon the student will lose interest because it is such a struggle. So have your children read on a daily basis.

Because learning to read does not end at the classroom door, parents need to model reading and have lots of reading material in the home. To encourage children, I have found that there should be a daily time for reading. They can select the material based on their interests. Reading is the ultimate goal. It is fun when everyone in the family reads together. Setting the kitchen timer for 15 to 20 minutes helps the reluctant reader know that there is a time limit and they will not be reading forever. Finish with a brief discussion of what was read to check for understanding and comprehension. Look for motivating library programs. Many bookstores also have reading times for children on the weekends with visiting readers and authors. This is a good way to encourage children to read more material that is intellectually stimulating and challenging.

I am frequently asked about the effect of television on reading. Watching television does take up time that children could spend reading. There are, however, some television shows that promote learning, such as programs about science, historical events, famous people, etc. Set a specific amount of time each week for television viewing and establish a list of approved programs. Try a week without TV. You will be surprised at how creative children can be with their time and how much you will enjoy their company.

Through reading we can give children a window of opportunity to grow and learn. With your help and motivation, the window will stay open, and you will see your children become lifelong readers in a literate society.

103

Family Reading and Writing: Let's Make it a Family Event!

By Beth Peller
Communication Arts Coordinator
Community School District 15 , Brooklyn, New York

Family Reading and Writing is a parent-involvement program developed by C.S.D. 15, located in Brooklyn, New York. This program was designed by teachers and reading specialists as a two-part approach: Family Literacy Workshops for parents and caregivers were conducted during the school day. These workshops highlighted book selection and read-aloud techniques. *Family Reading and Writing* workshops were also given in the evening for parents and children together. The format included several hands-on reading and writing activities, a read-aloud period, and plenty of time for questions and answers.

This program highlighted the fact that reading and writing are the keys to success for most children in school. All schoolwork tends to be less difficult for children who read and write with ease. You, as your child's first and continuing teacher, can help your child become a better reader and writer by:

- **Talking to your child:** Just about everyday activities and events in your home. The more words children hear, the easier it will be for children to use words and later to read them.

- **Listening to your child:** Encourage children to talk about things they see or do. Most children enjoy talking when they know someone is interested in what they have to say. Talking will increase vocabulary and help them to become better readers and writers.

Family Reading and Writing:
Let's Make it a Family Event!

(continued)

- **Reading to your child:** When children are read to, they learn that books can be fun, and they develop a desire to learn to read by themselves. Reading to their children may be one of the most important things parents can do.

- **Taking your child places:** Visit places such as museums, art galleries, airports, parks, zoos, and children's dance companies and theaters to help give children new interests. Children usually like to read and write about things they have seen.

- **Letting your child see you read and write:** Children should see parents enjoying reading and writing to help them develop an appreciation for these activities.

- **Encouraging your child to read to you:** Most children learning to read want to demonstrate their new ability to the people who mean the most to them, namely, their parents. So, when your child wants to read something to you, it is important that you take the time to listen.

- **Offering help if necessary:** If your child is just beginning to read, don't hesitate to help with words that cause difficulty. Later, you can offer suggestions for figuring out such words independently. One suggestion might be to have the child decide what a word is by looking at the picture on the page. Another suggestion might be to have the child skip over the unknown word, read the rest of the sentence, and then figure out the unknown word from the sense of the sentence.

- **Praising your child:** Learning to read is not as easy as the average adult reader thinks it is. A child needs encouragement, so praise your child for any success, however limited.

105

Family Reading and Writing: Let's Make it a Family Event!
(continued)

- **Being patient:** Your child may mispronounce or fail to recognize the same word many times, even though you keep supplying it. This is not unusual. If you are patient, sooner or later your child will learn the word. If you find you are getting angry or impatient, stop and do something else. A child who is scared, upset, or under pressure is less likely to learn than a child who is calm and unworried.

- **Not comparing your child to others:** Your child is a unique individual. It is not fair to compare any child to a brother, a sister, or a neighbor's child. Some children learn faster than others. If your child seems a bit slower than others, remember that it is not intentional on the part of the child. Make it clear at all times that you love your child for what he or she can do. Give praise for accomplishments, but don't criticize your child for not doing as well as others.

There are so many reasons to read **with** and **to** our children:
- Reading with your children sends a positive message: I want to spend time with you. Your child will carry that message forever.
- Reading aloud promotes good listening skills, and good listeners are good learners.
- Reading stretches imaginations, introduces new ideas, and encourages independent thinking.
- Reading at home gives your child an advantage in school. Children become better readers by reading.
- Reading means more than just books. Try reading license plates, billboards, road signs, etc.

REMEMBER: *Enthusiasm for reading is contagious!*

●●●●●●● **The Dewey Decimal System** ●●●●●●●

Teach your child the Dewey Decimal System of Classification to help him or her find books more easily in the library. Books are shelved under the following numbers and categories:

000–099 General Works
Bibliographies, General Encyclopedias, Reference Books

100–199 Philosophy and Psychology

200–299 Religion
Bible, Christian Religions, Other Religions, Greek and Roman Mythology

300–399 Social Science
Government, Community Life, Conservation, Transportation, Law, Holidays, Folk Tales, Fairy Tales and Legends, Costumes, Etiquette

400–499 Language
English Language, Study of Words, Alphabets, Dictionaries, Foreign Languages

500–599 Pure Sciences
Mathematics, Astronomy, Physics, Chemistry, Geology, Prehistoric Life, Living Things

600–699 Applied Sciences
Medical Sciences, Diet and Physical Fitness, Engineering, Electronics, Automobiles, Space and Aeronautics, Gardening, Pets, Cookbooks

700–799 Fine Arts
Music, Film, Television, Drawing, Painting, Photography, Architecture, Pottery, Coins, Handicrafts, Hobbies, Games, Sports, Magic

800–899 Literature
Poetry, Plays, Short Stories

900–999 History
History, Geography, Travel, Atlases, Collective Biographies

Raising Ravenous Readers
© The Learning Works, Inc.

 # The Parts of a Book

Kids will become more ravenous readers if they are familiar with the various parts of a book and understand the purpose of each section. Here are some new terms to introduce to your child. (Explain to your child that not all books have every section listed below.) Find a book in the library that contains most of the following pages or sections, and take time to talk about each page or section as you point it out in the book.

Half-Title Page The first printed page in a book and the page on which only the main part of the book title is listed. Both the subtitle and the author's name are omitted from this page.

Title Page The second printed page in a book and the page on which the full title of the book, the name of the author, the name of the illustrator, and the name of the publisher are listed.

author: the person who wrote the book.
illustrator: the person who created the pictures
publisher: the company or person who issued the book

Copyright Page Usually the back of the title page, this page includes the copyright notice, the name of the person or publishing company holding the copyright, and the year in which the book was copyrighted.

Dedication Page Page that carries a brief statement in which the author inscribes or addresses his book to someone as a way of recognizing or complimenting that person.

 **The Parts of a Book**
(continued)

Table of Contents   A list of the significant parts of a book by title and page number in the order in which they appear. It is usually near the front of the book and includes the introduction, all chapter titles, the bibliography, and the index (if there is one).

Preface   A statement by the author telling how or why he or she wrote the book and acknowledging any help he or she had in doing so.

Introduction   An essay that sets the scene for the book, explains the subject or format of the book, or tells how to use the book.

Body of Text   The main part of the book.

Notes   Additional explanatory information about facts in the text or about the sources from which they have been gathered.

Glossary   An alphabetical list of difficult, special, or technical words used in a book along with their definitions and, sometimes, their pronunciations.

Bibliography   A list of articles and other books referred to in the book or used by the author in writing it, or a list of writings relating to the same subject as the text. The works in a bibliography are usually arranged in alphabetical order based on the authors' last names.

Index   An alphabetical list of the names or topics covered in a book, together with the page numbers on which they are defined, explained, or discussed. The index usually appears at the end of the book.

Raising Ravenous Readers
© The Learning Works, Inc.

Checklist for Raising a Ravenous Reader

As a parent, there are many things you can do to raise a ravenous reader. Here is a checklist of ideas that will serve as a guide for helping your child develop a love of reading.

- Show your child you value books by reading to him or her for at least 20 minutes a day. Also make family time where each member spends time reading silently together instead of watching television.

- Fill a bookshelf in your child's room. Look for books at your favorite children's bookstore, at garage sales, or at bookstores that sell used books. By providing your child with his or her own library, you are sending the message that reading is important. It is also a great opportunity to teach your child how to properly care for books.

- Talk to your child about the books or stories he or she is reading. By asking questions, you show you care and are interested in his or her progress. When you ask your child what the book he or she is reading is about, you provide him or her with an opportunity to summarize the story and think about the central theme or idea.

- Discuss with your child the various feelings that characters in his or her book are experiencing. Have him or her recall specific details and events in the story that brought about these emotions. Ask your child if he or she has ever experienced these or similar feelings. This type of dialogue will help your child become a more sensitive reader. It will also serve as a springboard to some wonderful conversations about your child's own feelings and may provide you with new insights into your son or daughter.

- Take your child to the library on a regular basis. Encourage your son or daughter to talk to the children's librarian and get recommendations for books that best meet his or her needs. Take advantage of special programs your library offers throughout the year, such as guest children's authors, storytellers, plays, and puppet shows. Many public libraries also offer children's summer reading programs. This is a great way to make sure that your child doesn't fall behind over the summer.

Checklist for Raising a Ravenous Reader
(continued)

- Teach your child the importance of following written directions. Purchase a model appropriate for your child's age. Have him or her read the directions and use the illustrations provided to assemble the model. Be there to assist when needed, but have your child read and follow the directions as independently as possible. This activity will emphasize the importance of being able to read and follow written directions. Talk with your child about other times when it is necessary to read and follow directions, for example, when taking a test at school, reading the directions on a bottle of medicine, or following the steps in a recipe. Discuss the consequences if directions are misread or not followed properly.

- Give your child a subscription to a children's magazine as a holiday or birthday present. Today there are magazines on the market that appeal to nearly every child, from the nature lover to the sports enthusiast. Select a magazine to meet your own child's special interests. Most kids enjoy getting mail, and a subscription to a magazine is a gift of reading that will last throughout the year. For a list of children's magazines, see pages 118–122.

- Help increase your child's vocabulary as he or she reads. When your child comes to a word that is unfamiliar, break the word into smaller parts and have your child read the more familiar word sounds, such as any prefixes or suffixes. Help him or her sound out the rest of the word. Many board games are available at your local toy store or bookstore that provide reading and vocabulary reinforcement. Playing word games at home is a fun way to strengthen reading skills and build a stronger vocabulary.

- Help your child develop the skill of drawing conclusions as he or she reads. After reading a chapter of a favorite book, stop and ask your child what he or she thinks will happen next. Ask what facts were read in the chapter that helped him or him arrive at his or her conclusion. This skill teaches your child to make inferences based on facts that he or she has read. Then continue reading to see if your child's conclusions were right or wrong.

Raising Ravenous Readers
© The Learning Works, Inc.

Tips for Reading Aloud

1. After selecting a book to read to your child, take time to read it yourself first so you can judge whether it will appeal to your child's interests and is appropriate for his or her age level.

2. When reading to your child, read slowly and give your child time to visualize what you are reading. Use lots of expression in your voice to hold your child's attention.

3. Read to your child every opportunity you get. Read books while waiting in restaurants or doctors' offices, after dinner, during family vacations, at bedtime—anytime and anyplace!

4. Take time to discuss highlights of the book with your child.

5. Learn more about the author of the book you and your child are reading. Your library probably has a copy of *Something About the Author* which provides biographical information about well-known authors. This resource can also help you find other books written by your child's favorite authors.

6. When reading aloud, stop at a place in the book that will leave your child wanting to hear more the next day.

Reading aloud is a great opportunity to communicate with your child and to instill a love of reading and books.

Ways to Develop Rapid Readers

Kids need to learn how to read at different speeds or rates. Teaching your child *when* to use these different rates of reading and *how* to develop these different rates will help him or her in school.

A regular reading rate is ideal for pleasure reading or for finding answers to questions a teacher might ask. A slower rate of reading is necessary when studying and trying to memorize specific details for a test. Children also use a slower rate of reading when they take notes, put things in sequence, or try to memorize details for a test or quiz.

One thing you can do to help your child is to teach him or her how to read rapidly or skim words on a page. Teach your son or daughter how to look for key words in selections they read. These key words are usually nouns and verbs and give an overall idea of what the paragraph is about.

Also teach your child how to read in phrases rather than reading one word at a time. To provide practice, take a selection from a newspaper and divide it into phrases or groups of words. Have your child practice reading in this manner to improve his or her rate of reading, and to train his or her eyes to group and read more words at a time.

113

Raising Ravenous Readers
© The Learning Works, Inc.

Super Internet Sites for Ravenous Readers

Welcome to The Read In!
http://www.readin.org/

The Read In! is a one-day-a-year Internet event that helps children around the world talk to famous authors and to each other. The site is sponsored by the Read In Foundation, Inc., which promotes and encourages global literacy and the use of telecommunications technology in education.

(Copyright 1994–97 by The Read In!)

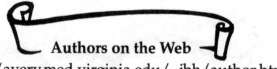

Learning to Love Reading: Maya Angelou
http://homearts.com/depts/family/mayab1.htm

Read this inspiring interview of Maya Angelou who answers the question, "What were some of the books that turned you into a lifelong lover of reading?" Read further to find Angelou's recommendations of books a person should read by the time he or she is 18.

(Copyright 1997 by The Hearst Corporation)

Authors on the Web
http://avery.med.virginia.edu/~jbh/author.html

This Web page brings together author biographies available on the World Wide Web. The creator of this site has also included a link to The Nobel Prize Internet Archive.

(This site was created by Bonnie Hanks, M.A., English, Duke University.)

Super Internet Sites for Ravenous Readers
(continued)

Tell Me More! Information About Children's Authors and Illustrators and Their Books
http://www.acs.ucalgary.ca/~dkbrown/authors.html

This Web site includes a long list of children's authors, Boys' and Girls' series Web pages, Oz books, information about folk tales, and more. Tell Me More! is a feature of The Children's Literature Web Guide, which can be found at:

http://www.ucalgary.ca/~dkbrown/index.html

(This site is organized by David K. Brown, Doucette Library of Teaching Resources, University of Calgary.)

Notable Books for Children
http://www.ala.org/alsc/notable97.html

Nearly 60 books are listed, each with a short review. The books are divided into sections for younger readers, middle readers, older readers, and all ages.

(Copyright 1997 by American Library Association)

Book Nook
http://i-site.on.ca/booknook.html

Book Nook is by kids and for kids, which means all the books are reviewed by children. After you have finished reading a book, write a review of it, post it, and look for it on this site. Parents can look at "Helping Your Child Learn to Read" by the U.S. Department of Education.

(This site is maintained by I-Site.on.Canada.)

Raising Ravenous Readers
© The Learning Works, Inc.

Super Internet Sites for Ravenous Readers
(continued)

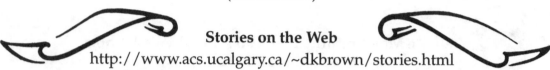

Stories on the Web
http://www.acs.ucalgary.ca/~dkbrown/stories.html

This Web site includes a variety of stories under these headings: Story Collections, Folklore, Myth and Legend, Songs and Poetry, Classics for Young People, and Contemporary Writing for Children and Young Adults. This site is a feature of The Children's Literature Web Guide which includes Lots of Lists, Recommended Books, Journals and Book Reviews, and Movies and Television Based on Children's Books.

(This site is organized by David K. Brown, Doucette Library of Teaching Resources, University of Calgary.)

Kids Web—Literature
http://www.npac.syr.edu/textbook/kidsweb/literature.html

At this site you can find links to Web pages under these categories: Children's Books, Creative Writing, Fiction, Poetry, Theater, and General Literature.

(This Web page is maintained by Paul Coddington, Northeast Parallel Architectures Center, Syracuse University.)

The Internet Public Library
http://www.ipl.org/youth/

Check out the Internet Public Library's cool stuff by clicking on these buttons: Reading Zone, Reference, Our World, Science Net, Fun Stuff, and more.

(This site is made possible by the collaborative efforts of teachers, librarians, and students, and the staff of the Internet Public Library.)

Super Internet Sites for Ravenous Readers
(continued)

Welcome to the Newbery Medal Home Page!
http://www.ala.org/alsc/newbery.html

Welcome to the Caldecott Medal Home Page!
http://www.ala.org/alsc/caldecott.html

How many Newbery or Caldecott Medal books have you read? Each of these sites gives a short history of the medals and how they are awarded, provides highlights of the most recent recipients, and gives a summary of each book. You can also find a list of all the winning books and authors since the inception of the awards.

(Created for the American Library Service to Children; copyrighted by the American Library Association.)

 **Tales to Tell**
http://www.thekids.com/kids/stories/

The stories at this site have illustrations and large, easy-to-read text. Story categories include Rhymes and Nonsense, Fables and Animal Stories, Stories from Everywhere, and Heroes and Adventures.

(This site was created by thekids.com.)

Tales of Wonder: Folk and Fairy Tales from Around the World
http://darsie.ucdavis.edu/tales/

The stories in this collection represent a sampling of the rich storytelling art that is the common heritage of humanity. You can find folk and fairy tales from Africa, Russia, Japan, England, Native America, India, and more.

(This site is owned by Richard Darsie.)

Raising Ravenous Readers
© The Learning Works, Inc.

Great Magazines for Kids

American Girl
Pleasant Company Publications, Inc.
8400 Fairway Place
Middleton, WI 53562
(Blend of historical fiction and nonfiction for girls age 7 and older)

Bananas
Scholastic, Inc.
730 Broadway
New York, NY 10003

Boys' Life
Boy Scouts of America
1325 Walnut Hill Lane
Irving, TX 75038-3096

Bugs Bunny Presents Looney Tunes Magazine
Welsh Publishing Group
300 Madison Avenue
New York, NY 10017-6216
(Bugs, Daffy, and the gang star in this magazine packed with zany games, comics, stories, and puzzles)

The Children's Album
EGW Publishing Company
Box 6086
Concord, CA 94524
(Stories, plays, poetry, crafts)

Cobblestone
Cobblestone Publishing, Inc.
20 Grove Street
Peterborough, NH 03458
(American history for young people ages 8–14)

Creative Kids (Chart Your Course)
GCT Inc.
Box 6448
Mobile, AL 36660-0448
(Original works of gifted, creative, and talented young people ages 5–18)

Cricket
Open Court Publishing Company
315 Fifth Street
Peru, IL 61354

Great Magazines for Kids

Disney Adventures
Walt Disney Publications
500 South Buena Vista
Burbank, CA 91521
(For young people ages 7–14; includes music, movies, trends, science, travel, gadgets, games, heroes, explorers, and more)

The Dolphin Log
The Cousteau Society
8440 Santa Monica Boulevard
Los Angeles, CA 90069

Dr. Jim's PETZINE for Kids
Good Dog!
P.O. Box 31292
Charleston, SC 29417
(A fun and educational monthly newsletter that helps kids learn about pets and responsible pet care)

Ebony, Jr.
820 South Michigan Avenue
Chicago, IL 60605

Faces: The Magazine About People
Cobblestone Publishing, Inc.
7 School Street
Peterborough, NH 03458-1470
(Cultural anthropology for young people age 8–15; published in cooperation with the American Museum of Natural History)

Fast Forward
Opportune Press
79 Walnut
Mill Valley, CA 94941
(By kids, for kids, and about kids growing up today)

Garfield Magazine
Welsh Publishing Group
300 Madison Avenue
New York, NY 10017-6216
(Quarterly magazine for children ages 6–12; includes stories, puzzles, jokes, and comics)

Highlights for Children
803 Church Street
Honesdale, PA 18431

Raising Ravenous Readers
© The Learning Works, Inc.

Great Magazines for Kids

Hopscotch, The Magazine for Girls
Bluffton News Publishing and Printing
    Company
Box 164
Bluffton, OH 45817-0164

Hot Dog
Scholastic, Inc.
730 Broadway
New York, NY 10003-9511

Jack and Jill
Children's Better Health Institute
1100 Waterway Boulevard
Indianapolis, IN 46202

Kid City (Electric Company)
Children's Television Workshop
1 Lincoln Plaza
New York, NY 10023-7129

Kids Discover
170 Fifth Avenue
New York, NY 10010
(For children ages 5–12; each issue covers a
single topic in nature, science, geography,
or man-made wonders)

MAD
E.C. Publications
485 MADison Avenue
New York, NY 10022
(Puzzles, games, and articles for children)

McMag
McDonald's Corporation
Publications Department
1 Kroc Drive
Oak Brook, IL 60521
(Puzzles, games, and articles for children)

Mickey Mouse
Welsh Publishing Group
300 Madison Avenue
New York, NY 10017-6216

Monkey Shines on America
N.C. Learning Institute for Fitness
    and Education
Box 10245
Greensboro, NC 27404-0245
(A children's magazine focusing on American
history, geography, folklore, people, etc.; each
issue covers a different state)

Great Magazines for Kids

Muppet Magazine
475 Park Avenue South
New York, NY 10016

National Geographic World
National Geographic Society
17th and M Streets, N.W.
Washington, D.C. 20036

News for Kids
D.M. Publishing, Inc.
400 Heliotrope Avenue
Corona Del Mar, CA 92625-2921
(A magazine for children ages 7–12;
encourages reader contributions)

Noah's Ark
7726 Portal
Houston, TX 77071
(A monthly newspaper about Jewish history,
holidays, and laws)

Odyssey
Kalmbach Publishing Company
1027 N. Seventh Street
Milwaukee, WI 53233
(For children ages 8–12; emphasizes
astronomy and outer space)

Owl Magazine
The Young Naturalist Foundation
56 The Esplanade, Suite 306
Toronto, Ontario M5E 1A7
Canada

ProAction
Marvel Entertainment Group
387 Park Avenue, South
New York, NY 10016-8810
(Combines comic strip characters with NFL
football stars; features sports and fashion news)

Ranger Rick
National Wildlife Federation
1412 16th Street, N.W.
Washington, D.C. 20036

Sports Illustrated for Kids
500 Office Park Drive
Birmingham, AL 35223

Stone Soup, the Magazine by Children
Children's Art Foundation
Box 83
Santa Cruz, CA 95063-0083
(A collection of poems, stories, book reviews,
and art by children age 13 and younger)

Raising Ravenous Readers
© The Learning Works, Inc.

Great Magazines for Kids

Storyworks
Scholastic, Inc.
555 Broadway
New York, NY 10012
(A literature-based magazine for children ages 8–11)

3-2-1 Contact
Children's Television Workshop
One Lincoln Plaza
New York, NY 10023

Wow
Scholastic, Inc.
730 Broadway
New York, NY 10003

Young American
(Newspaper for kids)
Young American Publishing Company
Box 12409
Portland, OR 97212

Young Author's Magazine
Theraplan, Incorporated
3015 Woodsdale Boulevard
Lincoln, NE 68502
(Features the work of gifted children)

Zillions (Penny Power)
Consumer Reports Books
9180 LeSaint Drive
Fairfield, OH 45014
(Consumer advice for young people ages 8–14 from Consumer Reports)

Zoobooks
930 W. Washington, Suite 6
San Diego, CA 92103

Newbery Medal Winners

The Newbery Medal is awarded each year by the American Library Association to the American author of the most distinguished contribution to literature for children. This medal is named for John Newbery (1713–1767), an English publisher and bookseller. When looking for a reliable list of good books for kids to read, Newbery Award-winning books are a good place to start.

Year	Title	Author
1922	*The Story of Mankind*	Hendrik Van Loon
1923	*The Voyages of Doctor Dolittle*	Hugh Lofting
1924	*The Dark Frigate*	Charles Hawes
1925	*Tales from Silver Lands*	Charles Finger
1926	*Shen of the Sea*	Arthur Chrisman
1927	*Smoky*	Will James
1928	*Gay-Neck, the Story of a Pigeon*	Dhan Gopal Mukerji
1929	*The Trumpeter of Krakow*	Eric P. Kelly
1930	*Hitty, Her First Hundred Years*	Rachel Field
1931	*The Cat Who Went to Heaven*	Elizabeth Coatsworth
1932	*Waterless Mountain*	Laura Adams Armer
1933	*Young Fu of the Upper Yangtze*	Elizabeth Coatsworth
1934	*Invincible Louisa*	Cornelia Meigs
1935	*Dobry*	Monica Shannon
1936	*Caddie Woodlawn*	Carol Brink
1937	*Roller Skates*	Ruth Sawyer

Raising Ravenous Readers
© The Learning Works, Inc.

Newbery Medal Winners
(continued)

Year	Title	Author
1938	*The White Stag*	Kate Seredy
1939	*Thimble Summer*	Elizabeth Enright
1940	*Daniel Boone*	James Daugherty
1941	*Call it Courage*	Armstrong Sperry
1942	*The Matchlock Gun*	Walter D. Edmonds
1943	*Adam of the Road*	Elizabeth Janet Gray
1944	*Johnny Tremain*	Esther Forbes
1945	*Rabbit Hill*	Robert Lawson
1946	*Strawberry Girl*	Lois Lenski
1947	*Miss Hickory*	Carolyn Sherwin Bailey
1948	*The Twenty-One Balloons*	William Pene du Bois
1949	*King of the Wind*	Marguerite Henry
1950	*The Door in the Wall*	Marguerite de Angeli
1951	*Amos Fortune, Free Man*	Elizabeth Yates
1952	*Ginger Pye*	Eleanor Estes
1953	*Secret of the Andes*	Ann Nolan Clark
1954	*. . . And Now Miguel*	Joseph Krumgold
1955	*The Wheel on the School*	Meindert DeJong
1956	*Carry on, Mr. Bowditch*	Jean Lee Latham
1957	*Miracles on Maple Hill*	Virginia Sorensen

Newbery Medal Winners
(continued)

Year	Title	Author
1958	*Rifles for Watie*	Harold V. Keith
1959	*The Witch of Blackbird Pond*	Elizabeth George Speare
1960	*Onion John*	Joseph Krumgold
1961	*Island of the Blue Dolphins*	Scott O'Dell
1962	*The Bronze Bow*	Elizabeth George Speare
1963	*A Wrinkle in Time*	Madeleine L'Engle
1964	*It's Like This, Cat*	Emily Neville
1965	*Shadow of a Bull*	Maia Wojciechowska
1966	*I, Juan de Pareja*	Elizabeth Borton de Trevino
1967	*Up a Road Slowly*	Irene Hunt
1968	*From the Mixed-Up Files of Mrs. Basil E. Frankweiler*	Elaine Konigsburg
1969	*The High King*	Lloyd Alexander
1970	*Sounder*	William H. Armstrong
1971	*The Summer of the Swans*	Betsy Byars
1972	*Mrs. Frisby and the Rats of NIMH*	Robert C. O'Brien
1973	*Julie of the Wolves*	Jean Craighead George
1974	*The Slave Dancer*	Paula Fox
1975	*M. C. Higgins, The Great*	Virginia Hamilton
1976	*The Grey King*	Susan Cooper

Raising Ravenous Readers
© The Learning Works, Inc.

Newbery Medal Winners

(continued)

Year	Title	Author
1977	*Roll of Thunder, Hear My Cry*	Mildred D. Taylor
1978	*Bridge to Terabithia*	Katherine Paterson
1979	*The Westing Game*	Ellen Raskin
1980	*A Gathering of Days: A New England Girl's Journal*	Joan Blos
1981	*Jacob Have I Loved*	Katherine Paterson
1982	*A Visit to William Blake's Inn*	Nancy Willard
1983	*Dicey's Song*	Cynthia Voigt
1984	*Dear Mr. Henshaw*	Beverly Cleary
1985	*The Hero and the Crown*	Robin McKinley
1986	*Sara, Plain and Tall*	Patricia MacLachlan
1987	*The Whipping Boy*	Sid Fleischman
1988	*Lincoln: A Photo-Biography*	Russell Freedman
1989	*Joyful Noise: Poems for Two Voices*	Paul Fleischman
1990	*Number the Stars*	Lois Lowry
1991	*Maniac Magee*	Jerry Spinelli
1992	*Shiloh*	Phyllis Naylor
1993	*Missing May*	Cynthia Rylant
1994	*The Giver*	Lois Lowry
1995	*Walk Two Moons*	Sharon Creech
1996	*The Midwife's Apprentice*	Karen Cushman
1997	*The View from Saturday*	E. L. Konigsburg
1998	*Out of the Dust*	Karen Hesse
1999	*Holes*	Louis Sachar

Books for Special Interests

Art and Artists

Bill Peet: An Autobiography, by Bill Peet. Houghton. A lively book by an illustrator who worked at Disney Studios for many years.

Drawing from Nature, by Jim Arnosky. Lothrup. An acclaimed book by a naturalist who has written several books on drawing for children.

Linnea in Monet's Garden, by Christina Bjork. Farrar. A young French girl, Linnea, learns about Monet and impressionism in this delightful book.

Astronomy

Astronomy Today, by Isaac Asimov. Stevens. An introductory volume to the series, "Isaac Asimov's Library of the Universe."

Einstein Anderson Tells a Comet's Tale, by Seymour Simon. Puffin. One in a series of mysteries about a 12-year-old detective.

Find the Constellations, by H. A. Rey. Houghton. Straightforward text and illustrations about the stars by the creator of *Curious George.*

Planetarium, by Barbara Brenner. Bantam. Take a tour of the solar system.

The Space Atlas, by Heather Couper and Nigel Henbest. Harcourt. A big book about the solar system, with lots of illustrations. Also see Couper and Henbest's excellent book, *Black Holes,* published by DK Books.

Raising Ravenous Readers
© The Learning Works, Inc.

Books for Special Interests

Aviation

Barnstormers and Daredevils, by K. C. Tessendorf. Macmillan. Exciting, true tales.

How an Airport Really Works, by George Sullivan. Dutton. The history of airports.

Lost Star: The Story of Amelia Earhart, by Patricia Lauber. Scholastic. A well-done biography.

Planes, Gliders, Helicopters and Other Flying Machines, by Terry Jennings. Kingfisher. Lots of illustrations and simple explanations.

The Wright Brothers: How They Invented the Airplane, by Russell Freedman. Holiday House. Their fascinating story told with text and photos.

Ballet

Anna Pavlova: Genius of the Dance, by Ellen Levine. Scholastic. An engaging biography of one of Russia's most acclaimed dancers.

Ballet Steps: Practice to Performance, by Antony Dufort. Crown. Explanations accompanied by text, diagrams, and photos.

Cynthia Gregory Dances Swan Lake, by Cynthia Gregory. Simon & Schuster. A photo essay about a ballerina.

Dance Me a Story: Twelve Tales from the Classic Ballet, by Jane Rosenberg. Thames & Hudson. Includes such favorites as *Swan Lake* and *Romeo and Juliet.*

Books for Special Interests

Baseball

Babe Ruth, by William R. Sanford and Carl R. Green. Macmillan. A biography complemented with photos.

The Great Baseball Card Hunt, by Daniel Greenberg. Simon & Schuster. A mystery from the "Southside Sluggers Baseball Mystery" series.

The Macmillan Book of Baseball Stories, by Terry Egan. Macmillan. Stories, poignant and true.

Stealing Home: The Story of Jackie Robinson. Scholastic. A biography of the national hero who broke the color barrier.

Cars and Trucks

Encyclopedia Brown's Book of Wacky Cars, by Donald J. Sobol. Morrow. The famed boy detective explores the world of cars and car trivia.

Here Come the Monster Trucks, by George Sullivan. Dutton. Monster trucks at work in auto arenas.

Michael Andretti at Indianapolis, by Michael Andretti. Simon & Schuster. What it's like to race at the Indy 500, as told by a master.

Renault Formula 1 Motor Racing Book. DK Books. Lots of color photographs and explanations.

Computers

Cybermania, by Alexandre Jardin. DK Books. In this fantasy full of illustrations, the Wren children enter a "virtual transporter" to hunt for family secrets inside a computer.

Grace Hopper: Programming Pioneer, by Nancy Whitelaw. Scientific American Books for Young Readers. The story of a key player in the early computer revolution, a female Navy officer.

Virtual Reality (book and 3-D Glasses), by H. P. Newquist. Scholastic. An intriguing look at the many possibilities offered by virtual reality.

Raising Ravenous Readers
© The Learning Works, Inc.

Books for Special Interests

Dinosaurs

Dinotopia: A Land Apart from Time, by James Gurney. HarperCollins. A wonderfully illustrated fantasy about a boy and his father who travel to a land cohabited by people and dinosaurs.

The Enormous Egg, by Oliver Butterworth. Little, Brown. A classic about a dinosaur hatched from a hen egg in New Hampshire, and the dilemma created for 12-year-old Nate.

The New Illustrated Dinosaur Dictionary, by Helen Roney Sattler. Lothrup. One of the best guides around.

Where to Find Dinosaurs Today, by Daniel and Susan Cohen. Dutton. An excellent guide for any enthusiast.

Disaster and Survival Stories

Catastrophe! Great Engineering Failure—and Success, by Alfred B. Bortz. Scientific American Books for Young Readers. This book discusses a variety of disasters, including the space shuttle *Challenger*, and how such situations might have been avoided.

Lost on a Mountain in Maine, by Donn Fendler. Beech Tree Books. The true story of a 12-year-old lost for nearly two weeks in 1939.

On Board the Titanic, by Shelley Tanaka. Hyperion. Illustrations, diagrams, photographs, and text tell the true story of two young survivors.

Gymnastics

Carol Johnston: The One-Armed Gymnast, by Pete Donovan. Childrens. An inspiring biography.

Gold Medal Glory: The Story of the 1996 Women's Gymnastic Team, by Daniel and Susan Cohen. Pocket Books. A biography of the young athletes who competed at the 1996 Olympic Games.

Jessica Goes for the Gold, by Francine Pascal. Bantam. The first novel in the Team Sweet Valley series, about a girl participating in a state competition.

Books for Special Interests

Heroes and Heroines

Four Against the Odds: The Struggle to Save Our Environment, by Stephen Krensky, Scholastic. Profiles of four conservationists: John Muir, Chico Mendes, Rachel Carson, and Lois Gibb.

People Who Make a Difference, by Brent Ashabranner, Dutton. Profiles 14 diverse individuals who have spent their lives helping others.

The Road from Home: A True Story of Courage, Survival, and Hope, by David Kherdian. Beech Tree. In this Newbery Honor Book, the author tells of his mother's experience during the Armenian holocaust in Turkey in 1915.

Horses

The Black Stallion, by Walter Farley. Random. A boy trains a wild Arabian stallion in this exciting, classic tale by a master of horse stories.

Horse, by Juliet Clutton-Brock. Knopf Eyewitness Books. Includes detailed anatomical drawings and diagrams.

Misty of Chincoteague, by Marguerite Henry. Macmillan. A classic, true tale told by one of the great writers of children's horse stories. Sequels are *Sea Star* and *Stormy, Misty's Foal.*

National Velvet, by Enid Bagnold. Avon. One of the most famous horse stories ever written.

Music

The Facts and Fictions of Minna Pratt, by Patricia MacLachlan. Harper & Row. Minna Pratt, a cello player, searches for answers about love and life in this excellent novel.

The Kids' World Almanac of Music: From Rock to Bach, by Elyse Sommer. Pharos. All sorts of facts and anecdotes.

A Young Person's Guide to Music, by Neil Ardley. DK Books. A book and CD-ROM, produced in association with the BBC Orchestra. A super resource for reading and listening.

Raising Ravenous Readers
© The Learning Works, Inc.

Books for Special Interests

Native Americans

A Boy Becomes a Man at Wounded Knee, by Ted Wood and Wanbli Numpa Afraid of Hawk. Walker. Excellent photo-essay about an 8-year-old Lakota boy who, along with his tribe, relives his ancestors' journey to Wounded Knee.

The Encyclopedia of Native America, by Trudy Griffin-Pierce. Viking. A fascinating history with lots of photos and illustrations.

The Sign of the Beaver, by Elizabeth George Speare. Houghton. A classic about an 18th-century boy who survives in Maine with the help of natives.

Soccer

Make the Team, Soccer: A Heads-Up Guide to Super Soccer! by Richard J. Brenner. Little. Step-by-step skills for beginners.

Pele: The King of Soccer, by Caroline Arnold. Watts. A biography of one of the world's greatest players.

The World Cup, by Michael Goodman. Creative Editions. An illustrated history from the "Great Moments in Sports" series.

Space Exploration

The Day We Walked on the Moon: A Photo History of Space Exploration. Scholastic. A history of the U.S. space program.

Judith Resnick, by Joanne E. Bernstein and Rose Blue. Dutton. Biography of a Jewish girl who grows up to be an astronaut.

Space: Look Inside Cross-Sections. DK Books. Up-close looks inside 12 spacecraft.

Space Camp: The Great Adventure for NASA Hopefuls, by Anne Baird. Morrow. A group of children spend six days at the U.S. Space Camp in Huntsville, Alabama.

 # Issue-Related Book List

Alcohol

Alcohol, by Pamela Holmes. Raintree. Part of a series, "Drugs—The Complete Story."

Hannah In Between, by Colby Rodowsky. Dell. Twelve-year-old Hannah copes with her alcoholic mother.

Not My Family: Sharing the Truth about Alcoholism, by Maxine B. Rosenberg. Macmillan. Interviews with children of alcoholic parents.

Death

How It Feels When a Parent Dies, by Jill Krementz. Knopf. Children who have lost a parent are interviewed and photographed in this honest account.

Bridge to Terabithia, by Katherine Paterson. Crowell. In one of the best books in children's literature, 10-year-old Jesse loses his best friend, Leslie.

Part of Me Died Too: Stories of Creative Survival Among Bereaved Children and Teenagers, by Virginia Lynn Fry. Dutton. Stories of children and teenagers who have lost parents and friends through illness, suicide, murder, and AIDS. A powerful book.

A Summer to Die, by Lois Lowry. Bantam. Meg, 13, must cope with the illness and death of her pretty and popular older sister.

Divorce

It's Not the End of the World, by Judy Blume. Dell. Twelve-year-old Karen tries to reconcile her parents, who are about to divorce, but the plot doesn't work.

Living with a Single Parent, by Maxine B. Rosenberg. Macmillan. Children ages 8–13 are interviewed about their experiences.

My Mother Got Married (and Other Disasters), by Barbara Parks. Knopf. Twelve-year-old Charles isn't happy with his new stepfamily.

Raising Ravenous Readers
© The Learning Works, Inc.

 # Issue-Related Book List

Domestic Violence

Almost a Hero, by John Neufeld. Athenium Books for Young Readers. Twelve-year-old Ben tries to rescue a homeless child who is being abused.

Child Abuse, by Gail B. Stewart. Macmillan. A discussion that includes facts as well as the true stories of several young adults.

What Jamie Saw, by Carolyn Coman. Front Street. In this Newbery Honor Book, nine-year-old Jamie lives a frightened life after fleeing his mother's violent boyfriend.

Drugs

Drugs and You, by Arnold Madison. Simon & Schuster. A discussion of drug use and abuse.

A Hero Ain't Nothin' But a Sandwich, by Alice Childress. Avon. In this book for older readers, 13-year-old Benjie, an African American, is hooked on drugs. The author uses dialect in this story of urban drugs.

Know about Drugs, by Margaret O. Hyde. Walker. Part of the "Know about" series, a discussion of the U.S. drug scene.

Say No and Know Why: Kids Learn about Drugs, by Wendy Wax. Walker. A nurse and an assistant district attorney visit a sixth-grade class in the Bronx to discuss drug problems.

 # Issue-Related Book List

Illness

How It Feels To Fight for Your Life, by Jill Krementz. Little. Interviews with 14 children, ages 7–16, who have had life-threatening diseases.

I Am the Universe, by Barbara Corcoran. Macmillan. A 13-year-old girl's mother is diagnosed with a brain tumor.

Understanding Cancer, by Susan N. Terkel and Marlene Lupiloff-Brazz. Watts. The disease, treatments, and a discussion of how to react when family or friends are diagnosed.

Moving

Amber Brown Is Not a Crayon, by Paula Danziger. Little. In the first of a delightful series, third-grader Amber must say good-bye to her best friend, Justin, who is moving.

Hold Fast to Dreams, by Andrea Davis Pinkney. Morrow. Twelve-year-old Deirdre, an African-American, moves from Baltimore to suburban Connecticut, where she experiences prejudice.

The Kid in the Red Jacket, by Barbara Parks. Knopf. Ten-year-old Howard moves from Massachusetts to Arizona.

School Stories

The Cat Ate My Gymsuit, by Paula Danziger. Delacorte. Marcy is bored by school, but tries to help a kind teacher who gets fired.

The Flunking of Joshua T. Bates, by Susan Richards Shreve. Knopf. Joshua has to repeat third grade, but he has a nice teacher who helps him.

Harriet the Spy, by Louise Fitzhugh. Harper & Row. In this classic, sixth-grader Harriet becomes an outcast after her classmates discover she has been spying on them.

Raising Ravenous Readers
© The Learning Works, Inc.

 **Issue-Related Book List**

Sexual Abuse

Feeling Safe, Feeling Strong: How to Avoid Sexual Abuse and What to Do If It Happens to You, by Susan Neiburg Terkel. Lerner. Six stories about children experiencing abuse ranging from obscene phone calls to incest, followed by facts and discussion.

I Hadn't Meant to Tell You This, by Jacqueline Woodson. Delacorte. Eighth-grader Marie discovers that her friend is being sexually abused by her father.

People, Love, Sex, and Families: Answers to Questions That Preteens Ask, by Eric W. Johnson. Information on many topics, including sexual abuse and incest.

Tolerance

Children Just Like Me: A Unique Celebration of Children Around the World, by Barnabas and Anabel Kindersley. DK Books. This joint project with UNICEF introduces readers and their families to real children all around the world, with interesting details and excellent photographs.

The Great Gilly Hopkins, by Katherine Paterson. Crowell. Eleven-year-old Gilly seems to be an unlovable and obnoxious bully until she meets Mrs. Trotter, her foster mother.

Thief of Hearts, by Lawrence Yep. HarperCollins. Stacey, of Chinese descent, is forced to befriend a new girl from China, who turns out to be unfriendly and difficult.

The Watsons Go to Birmingham—1963, by Christopher Paul Curtis. Delacorte. In this humorous and poignant Newbery Honor Book, an African-American family visits Grandma in Alabama in 1963.

Create a Book Club

Organize a book club for your child and a small group of his or her friends. The group can meet once a month to discuss a book everyone has read in advance. Keep the discussions short and lively. Everyone will enjoy hearing their peers' reactions and opinions to the book.

Below are some starter questions you can toss out to the group to get them going, but let the kids set the pace, tone, and direction of the discussions. (Older kids can lead their own discussions.)

- Why do you think the author chose this title for the book?

- When and where does the story take place?

- In what ways does the main character change from the beginning of the book to the end?

Raising Ravenous Readers
© The Learning Works, Inc.

Reading Coupons

Reproduce the reading coupons on pages 138 and 139. Use them as rewards for ravenous readers.

Good for an extra 15 minutes of reading at bedtime.	Good for an extra 30 minutes of reading at bedtime.
Good for a new paperback book of your choice.	Good for a new hardback book of your choice.

Reading Coupons

Reproduce the reading coupons on pages 138 and 139. Use them as rewards for ravenous readers.

Good for a
free movie rental
of a title you have
just read.

Good for
a comic book
of your choice.

Good for a trip
to your
favorite bookstore
to browse.

Good for
a magazine
of your choice.

Raising Ravenous Readers
© The Learning Works, Inc.

Ways to Reward Reading

Here are some fun ways to celebrate when
your son or daughter has finished reading a book.

- Reproduce the reading card below. Punch a hole or color in a square each time a book is completed. When the entire card is filled, treat your child to a book of his or her choice at your favorite school supply store or bookstore.

- Tie in a theme of a book your child has completed with a special event in your home. For example, if your child finishes reading *Alice in Wonderland*, celebrate with a tea party. If your child reads *Julie of the Wolves*, celebrate with snow cones.

Come up with your own creative tie-ins for books your child reads.
You can even create birthday parties based on a book the kids have read.

Finishing Touches

When your child finishes reading a book, there are a lot of fun things he or she can do, either alone or as a family project. Give some of these ideas a try. Have
 your child . . .

- Design a bookmark that tells something about the story.

- Make a word search puzzle using new words learned from reading the story.

- Draw a cartoon comic strip of the important events in the story.

- Using a wire coat hanger and string, create a mobile based on the book.

- Make a puppet to represent a character in the book.

- Make a crossword puzzle for a family member using words found in the story.

- Design and color a poster to advertise the book.

- Be creative and write a different ending to the story.

Raising Ravenous Readers
© The Learning Works, Inc.

 **Answer Key**

Page 62 • Poetry

1. B 2. E 3. D 4. F 5. A 6. C

Page 70 • What's What?

Birds	Mammals
auk	addax
jackdaw	agouti
kiwi	chamois
osprey	dingo
plover	eland
ptarmigan	koala
puffin	shrew
quetzal	tapir
rhea	vole
rook	wolverine
snipe	wombat
vireo	zebu

Page 71 • People and Places

People	Places
1. the sewing machine	1. Utah
2. 1890	2. Pacific Ocean
3. Cullen	3. Japan
4. penicillin	4. Italy
5. Thomas Chippendale	5. Society Islands

Page 72 • What Would You Do With?

1. wear
2. ride in
3. ride
4. plant
5. eat
6. measure
7. wear
8. play

Page 73 • Where Would You Find?

1. in your mouth
2. in a cave
3. in the zoo
4. on the ceiling
5. in your body
6. on the ground
7. in a grocery store
8. in the ground

Page 75 • Cross-Reference Review

1. E   7. B
2. K   8. F
3. I   9. H
4. L   10. C
5. A   11. G
6. J   12. D

Answer Key

Page 76 • Key Word Clues

1. Lincoln, Abraham
2. advertising
3. insects
4. Greece
5. Israel or holidays
6. dog
7. Austria or music
8. flight or transportation

Page 78 • Super Trivia Search

1. 1974
2. Esther Pauline "Eppie" Friedman Lederer
3. 3,000
4. 10,000°F
5. *Our American Cousin*
6. 186,282 miles per second
7. the brown pelican
8. a village in Wales

Page 79 • Claim to Fame

1.	D	7.	E
2.	I	8.	J
3.	K	9.	G
4.	A	10.	B
5.	L	11.	F
6.	H	12.	C

Page 87 • In-Betweeners

1.	West Virginia	9.	Georgia
2.	Nevada	10.	New Hampshire
3.	New Mexico	11.	Virginia
4.	South Dakota	12.	Indiana
5.	Missouri	13.	Arkansas
6.	South Carolina	14.	Iowa
7.	Nebraska	15.	North Carolina
8.	Utah		

Page 88 • How Many?

1. 2
2. 3
3. 4
4. 18
5. 5
6. 12
7. 2
8. 5

Page 89 • Which Sea?

1.	Sea of Japan	6.	Red Sea
2.	Aegean Sea	7.	Baltic Sea
3.	Caribbean Sea	8.	North Sea
4.	Dead Sea	9.	Yellow Sea
5.	Labrador Sea	10.	Arabian Sea

Raising Ravenous Readers
© The Learning Works, Inc.

Index